S [illegible] plores:

Th [illegible] boundaries
The boundaries between [illegible] elf and other
The nature of boundaries in the world around us
and
The fictionalizing of autobiographical stories
Writing exercises to stimulate the imagination

Monica Suswin's writing feels like a wise and trusted friend, whispering in our ear that *it'll be ok, perhaps try it this way?* She doesn't preach, but instead generously shares her own experiences to allow the reader to explore their own memories and feelings through a series of practical creative exercises, including letters, fiction, metaphors, and animal or dream imagery. *Shifting Boundaries* is an important book, one that should be kept near every writing journal, ready to pull out whenever we need inspiration.

Sarah Salway, poet, novelist,
tutor and practitioner in Writing and Wellbeing

Monica takes *Shifting Boundaries* as her broad subject and fearlessly dives into the muscular topics of life: love, death, sex and relationships. Her diaries and dreams guide us into these realms with agility, time travelling and nimbly changing perspective. She integrates the past to perceive the present with authenticity and transparency. Monica's passion for the art of writing is infectious and fuels my hunger to tell my story: to be known, to know myself.

Sarah Davies,
practitioner in Mindful Movement: Open Floor International

An inspiring and gently practical book to help transform experiences through the practice of writing. Creative prompts and rich storytelling uncover new insights and invite us ever deeper into memory and imagination.

Casper ter Kuile, author of *The Power of Ritual: Turning Everyday Activities into Soulful Practices* (2020, HarperOne)

Shifting Boundaries

creative therapeutic writing
on
family life and friendship

MONICA SUSWIN

for Julie
with much
love & affection
Monica

Forest Row
visit
20:iv:2023

CABIN PRESS

Published by Cabin Press 2020

Copyright © Monica Suswin 2020

Monica Suswin has asserted her right under the Copyright, Designs and Patents Act 1988, to be identified as the author of this work.

ISBN 978-0-9956882-2-3

This book is sold subject to the condition that it shall not, by way of trade or otherwise, be lent, resold, hired out, or otherwise circulated without the author's prior consent in any form of binding or cover other than that in which it is published.

Image of armadillo by Olivia Haughton
Author photograph by Daniel Regan

Printed in Great Britain by Short Run Press Ltd, Exeter

Shifting Boundaries
is dedicated to
Rosemary Luling Haughton

Nobody who has not been in the interior of a family, can say what the difficulties of any individual of that family may be.

Jane Austen
(Emma Ch.18, p.125)

We must take care of our families wherever we find them.

Elizabeth Gilbert

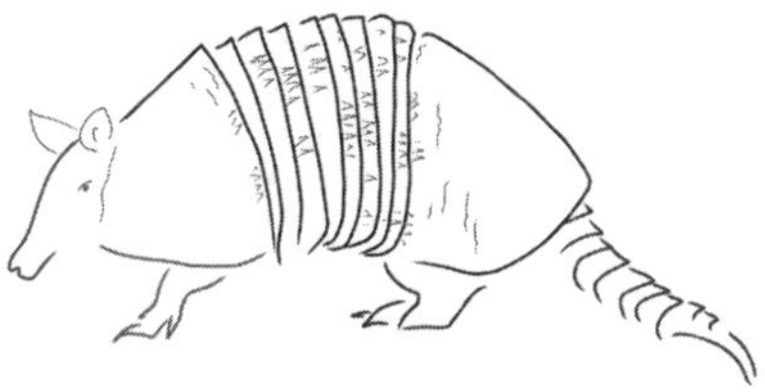

Imagination is more important than knowledge.
Knowledge is limited.
Imagination encircles the world.

Albert Einstein

All real living is meeting

Martin Buber

Contents

Foreword

Personal explorative writing is an adventure in every way: exhilarating and communicative at times, but sometimes scary and lonely. Monica, in her books, offers a treasure map to guide and help us venture sufficiently safely and confidently. In order not to lose ourselves, we need to maintain our integrity, our wholeness. In this volume, she helps us maintain our personal integrity in order to remain strong and flexible throughout dynamic writing explorations. We do this by being aware and careful of our boundaries – the edges of our wholeness where we meet other people and other experiences – some new and challenging. Lucy, right at the beginning of C.S. Lewis' 'Narnia' stories, crosses a boundary into an imaginative world where she will learn skills and wisdom to deal with her problematic real-life. She does it by simply pushing past fur coats towards the back of a wardrobe. Adventure, in the best stories, is a metaphor for the process of learning.

> Next moment [Lucy] found that what was rubbing against her face was not the soft fur of the coats, but the branches of trees. And then she saw that there was a light ahead of her; not a few inches away where the back of the wardrobe ought to have been, but a long way off.
>
> Lucy felt a little frightened, but she felt very inquisitive and excited as well. She looked back over her shoulder and there,

between the dark tree trunks, she could still see the open doorway of the wardrobe. She had, of course, left the door open. She began to walk forward, *crunch-crunch* over the snow and through the wood towards the other light.

Condensed from C.S. Lewis
The Lion, the Witch and the Wardrobe.
(1950) [2000]. London: Harper Collins. p.77

By walking through a wardrobe, Lucy discovered a new way of understanding and being. Writing is rather like that, except we use pen and paper (or words on a screen) to enter the imaginative world. We share her willingness to take those 'two or three steps', and then some more, through snow perhaps, or mud, or sun-warmed sea-water. Slowly the everyday world recedes, though the door we came through is always open for an easy return. Through writing we cross a boundary into our huge and wonderful creative beings, we 'walk forward towards the other light'.

This makes it sound easy. It isn't. Lucy took huge courage to start her adventure. She also didn't get far alone, but quickly met others who knew some of the paths. Monica, in her books, holds out her hand to help us find the necessary strength, and our individual way, in this strange and extraordinary land of writing. She is a reliable guide, having undertaken herself everything she suggests we do. And she illuminates the journey, helping us to understand by sharing her own writing and telling how she gained from it.

Early on in her personal explorations Monica needed security and confidence in her relationship with writing, to know that it was safely bounded. Without articulating this to herself, in her journal she crossed into the imaginative world, writing as a little girl playing house with a little girl friend. She says of that experience: 'The mud igloo story was a landmark in my imaginative writing. Solid and indestructible. I had built a safe home in my own mind. No-one could pull down lisa and dot's mud igloo. Because no-one could reach it. Because no-one knew where it was.' We can all 'build' ourselves a safe home for our writing; I have a mansion with lovely rooms and gardens for others to visit and share with me, and a hidden staircase to the totally private upstairs floors of imaginative adventure.

Monica's treasure map supports us to believe in ourselves and trust our writing hands. It helps us respect the writing process, even when it seems an odd, or even initially painful, activity. With this trust and respect we can adventure with integrity, with secure boundaries in place. We might meet witches and fauns, or fight dragons and win their gold and jewels. We will learn essential wisdom about ourselves and our lives.

Dr Gillie Bolton
Derbyshire, UK
June 2020

Gillie Bolton enjoys being fully retired, working on her own writing in Hope Valley, Derbyshire and Bloomsbury, London, and being grandmother to three wonderful young people.

Acknowledgements

Within the extensive boundary of my friends, family and clients I have been encouraged with this book. In particular, I thank my writing friends: Liz Bahs and Alison Bell, both of whom provide me with wise advice and live at opposite ends of the country – there are few opportunities for actual meetings, but optic fibres and satellite connections allow these geographical boundaries to be crossed.

My warmest thanks to Guy Jones and Patrick Jones for allowing me to use their mum's last piece about dying in the hospice. Sally stimulated my first published chapter *A Legacy of Understanding* in *Dying Bereavement and the Healing Arts* (2008, JKP) after she used a piece about my father dying to illustrate a lecture for student nurses at Barnet College, London. I miss her friendship deeply.

My thanks to Hrvojka Kostelic-Swift for being the best neighbour anyone could wish for the other side of a party wall – her puddings and cakes are much appreciated. The poem *Gifts* arose from her melt-in-the-mouth biscuits. A special thank you to Sarah Davies and our wonderful Open Floor dancing community where I have often explored my boundaries through awareness of our embodied energies in movement.

Thanks are due to Lulah Ellender as she grappled with boundaries and spaces in my document pages as the ether transfer shifted words most weirdly. And to Paul Luffman at Short Run Press who worked on the manuscript in between furlough weeks during the lockdown. I am grateful to Jane Flude for information from her family archives about our maternal grandmother.

My thanks to Rose Akroyd for her close reading at the eleventh hour.

My gratitude and thanks to Mark Haughton who made us all aware of how important tables are in family life. He made our dining table from apple and pear wood from the 1987 storm, the year our daughter was born. All the comments in Chapter 4 on the table's patina and its function in everyday life come from his words. I deeply thank Rosemary Haughton who welcomed me into her family some forty years ago and who has always, together with Nancy Schwoyer, been supportive of my writing adventure. They are both family and friends.

Animals have been wonderful metaphors in this series for both writing and illustration. I thank Olivia Haughton, who has humoured and delighted her mum with her drawings. And for making the armadillo such an endearing creature. Thanks are also due to Dr Christopher Willis for checking the accuracy – in lay terms – of my limited scientific knowledge. I should also thank my cat Zim for allowing me some access to my key-board when she didn't pad her way over the alphabet. Any typos are definitely feline.

Dr Gillie Bolton has opened my eyes to the wide shores and horizons of boundaries. I feel an abundance of *limitless* gratitude to her for being both editor and friend during this long process of writing. Without her this series of books would never have crossed the threshold into publication.

Introduction

Creative and therapeutic writing can help us understand different approaches to those we love, and perhaps those we do not love so much.

Shifting Boundaries is the third book in the series. It concerns how boundaries range from the visible ones in the landscape and cities around us to the invisible ones within the self and our friendships. The writing explores how the issues which crop up in family and friendships can shift and transform the interiority of our feelings so we live better lives, so we can become more aware of how our boundaries influence us. And how writing can help us achieve a fluidity in how we approach others.

During one of my trips to Morocco, I was asked if I lived inside or outside the *medina* in my Sussex village. Those are the town walls built as a defence and a statement to the outside world about the boundary of that place. Of course our village has no *medina*, but I could have mentioned that my front garden has a very high, thick coniferous hedge planted probably when the house was built. That provides me with a fixed boundary to the outside world. A hedge about eight feet high and several feet thick. Under an arch, through the gate, a path leads to the front door. Once inside I feel a comforting safety within the boundaries of my home's four outer walls.

Boundaries are not necessarily rigid as the title of the book suggests. Here I explore how my perception of boundaries has expanded through writing. I have found defining my own boundaries has sharpened my awareness of how I handle them, and how the inner boundaries of emotions shift around when I write. It has also made me notice what might be the boundaries I perceive around other people in my life. And how writing has helped to shift feelings about others. This has helped me relate more authentically.

There is one threshold we cross only once in our lives, and that is when we die. In *Dream Snatcher*, my parents (long-dead) visited me in a dream. My exploratory writing looked at the reasons we moved to different houses. Mine was a sea-house, whilst they lived nearby in a house for the dead. In this symbolic dream I owned my individual, adult identity, I wrote about my emotional separation from parents who had left their imprint (as all parents do) within the psychological boundaries of my inner self.

The transition from life to death extends into the second chapter, *Shifting Boundaries* as I write about the death of a friend finding peace as she faces the end of her life. I found it illuminating tracing how my own personal boundaries had evolved from childhood to the present. Time itself gives an overview of how the process of becoming oneself shifts through the years.

Observational writing found many fixed boundaries in the landscape and world around me. I looked for boundaries to scribble about in my notebook whilst walking the streets of London, and along the beaches in Norfolk. I wrote about s*hifting boundaries* when travelling up the Norwegian Coast to reach the Arctic Circle. And when I thought about the universe or the galaxy we live in, I found no boundaries at all.

Wall Fictions, the third chapter, explores relationships and emotional truths. Metaphor is a marvellous strategy to bring insights, increased awareness and clarity to personal writing. In *Wall Fictions,* the wall became my metaphor. Its plasticity to become various types of wall in my imagination helped me write about three types of relationship with different qualities of boundary. One with frustrated anger, one as a recognition of a close friendship and one showing that I do love myself.

With this writing, I also discovered a flow through experimenting with the voice of my inner little girl. Imaginatively she used mud to make bricks and build a *mud igloo* which started out as a form of playful writing, but still was underpinned by emotional truths and insights.

The fourth chapter *Tablecloth Talk* is about a family event, a birthday celebration. Writing a fiction from a real life event felt like crossing narrative boundaries. Scenario and characters were invented but again I stayed true to the feelings and found new insights knocked me sideways. The emotional parallels in the fictional narrative were surprisingly satisfying and unexpectedly cleared any discomfort left by the original real-life event itself.

The armadillo (see Chapter 2) protects the soft interiority of its body with hard shield-shaped scales. Any person may raise up invisible defences to protect their inner hurts and vulnerabilities. The great thing about any therapeutic practice is we can begin to heal the early hurts we may have experienced. That does not mean getting rid of them or the memories (we cannot do that). Sometimes those hurts may have been pre-verbal, before memories were laid down in the mind. But the body remembers.

In my own life, I have acknowledged the hurts of childhood, adolescence and family life. Psychotherapy when a younger adult, expressive writing and dance have all contributed to making my boundaries more secure, safer and agile in emotional shifts which help me live a good life. When I was in my twenties, I made a profound decision on recovering from my first serious clinical depression to do the best I could with my life. That best involves relating from a place of loving people and life. And I am particularly aware of the philosopher Martin Buber's contribution to understanding the spaces which exist in relationship. And the kind of flexibility they invoke in my consciousness. (see note on Buber p.108).

After I published the second book, *Love and Loss*, I felt that I could have renamed it *Love and Gain*. All my losses were held in love, and the process of writing. I felt profound gratitude that I could turn my experiences of loss into an act of creativity; writing so that others might read my book.

Writing goes a long way in teaching me how to give myself safe boundaries and take care of myself. It allows me to be a good friend to myself. And in turn means I can be a better companion to the friends I make in life. Above all I know that feelings may shift emotional boundaries with exploratory writing. Publishing a book is a form of reaching out beyond the boundaries of those people we know. Writing shifts the boundaries. For the writer and the reader.

THE SERIES

Shifting Boundaries: creative therapeutic writing on family life and friendships is the third book in this series. Each of the four books stands alone on a different theme.

Shifting Boundaries is for anyone interested in writing and its creative and therapeutic potential to explore their own sense of boundaries.

Shifting Boundaries is for all practitioners in the healing arts to examine that space between *self* and *other* in their practice.

Shifting Boundaries is for fledgling writers wanting to make fictions of their own personal narratives.

Each chapter ends with writing exercises based on the different styles and approaches in this book.

* An asterisk in the text indicates more information in the Notes.

CHAPTER 1

Dream Snatcher

CHILDHOOD HOMES

In my dreams, I am often on long involved journeys to the house where I grew up by the sea on the Essex coast, or to one of my grandparents' flats in London. All my grandparents have been dead for around forty years, yet in my dreams I am often on an intense search to find my way to one, or the other of their flats.

There is always an urgency to move in, as I have nowhere to live in London and I cannot go back to the flat in Kilburn I lived in during the eighties. I visit that flat too, but it is always occupied and altered architecturally, and it is always clear I cannot move back there. These are very anxious dreams, and I am glad to wake up safe in my bed in Sussex with the knowledge that this house, which I have lived in for twenty five years, is certainly where I feel settled, contained and happy.

The dream writing I explore in this chapter is not about any of the places I lived in during childhood or my younger years and often dream about. I write about a dream house which, given the chance, I would gladly live in because it gives me both a feeling of safety and excitement.

My dream was about moving to a new house with my mother and father in a setting I knew nothing about at all. The accommodation for me, I was surprised to learn, was some distance from the place for my mother and father. Although my parents are no longer alive, they continue their invisible lives in my sleeping hours. My exploratory writing made this dream house feel real and solid in my imagination.

THE LONG SEA HOUSE

The dream is recorded in the past tense, as I wrote it down in my diary first thing in the morning. Although as I describe my feelings whilst dreaming, I move to the present tense. It felt a little like a lucid dream, one that I was aware of as I dreamt, and in the morning the writing flowed.

The Dream

I have moved house with my parents. The estate agents omitted to tell us that part of the house is actually two hundred yards away. Down the same street, over a cross-road.

I walk over there. My living space is at the top of a complex condominium. I climb an external staircase and enter a room, which becomes longer as I move down it. The space is in two halves with low ceilings, and windows along both sides. There is no bathroom, no kitchen, just this long rectangular room.

As I reach the end of the room, I am looking out onto the sea, dunes and marshes. There is no end wall. I can walk straight out onto a hillside; to the left is a pathway leading down to a spit of land. The waves hit it on all sides.

I am excited. Only this room. No facilities. Although I am meant to be living with The Parents, they are in the other part of the house, over the cross-road. This is a separate place to live. I know I can live here and I want to. I know this as I dream.

At the far end overlooking the sea, where I had noticed no end to the room, I now see a sliding semi-circular concertina door to pull across the opening. I know it has never been pulled across. It is a marvellous room leading me to the sea, waves, light.

That is exactly how I experienced the sensations as I dreamt, and on waking I felt I had found the perfect room that suited me. It gave me the seascape I love and do not have, as in reality I live in semi-urban countryside. I wished I had such a house, I wished I could get into my car and drive to this one. On re-reading my description, however many years later, I always feel as if I am entering this dream space afresh. And experience an exhilaration about what I know the exploratory writing will uncover.

This dream revealed a strong sense of myself as apart from my parents. That much was obvious with the reality of their deaths. When they were alive, I had done so much writing about my relationship with them that it was not my concern to explore further my feelings as their daughter. I had done more than enough in the past.

EXPLORATORY WRITING

In my diary write-up there were a couple of phrases and sentences that jumped out at me, and which I wanted to explore. Using these as prompts is a tactic I often use. Having lifted the words I wanted, I then rewrote them, slightly altering the phrases and order from the original sentences. Then I had specific pointers from these dream snatches* to use as triggers to kickstart my writing.

Here is the first prompt. I worked with the word *cross* as a pun:

> *With parents! Over a cross-road.*
>
> Yes I have crossed the road at last away from you both. I can cross back and visit. But I live over the cross-road, not only in the land of the living but in a room with a sea-view to die for. Yet I am alive, and you are both dead. You can both live in that house you bought and manage on your own as best you can, and I will visit daily to check up on you.
>
> It was a cross road that we travelled together. Underlying anger on both sides. From you that I was not the daughter you might have wished for. From me that you were not the parents I might have wished for. Yet along the way (if rather late in our time together) came acceptance, and appreciation. And finally love for you both.

My mother lived in a nursing home for six years after my father died. When she succumbed to vascular dementia, it was apparent that the physical pain she had suffered all her adult life miraculously went. She became content and sweet, especially to the nursing staff. I was in the swimming pool with friends when my husband got the phone call to come in quickly. By the time he picked me up and we arrived (my hair still dripping wet), she had died. I wrote this poem soon after.

Smile

We kissed your forehead
colder than we could ever imagine
clipped a lock of silver grey hair

Sister Carmel told us:
how you smiled
how the blood fled back to your heart
exactly how your breath   stopped.

And Sister Carmel told us:
                                        how she placed
the golden rose in your clasped warm hands.

We sat vigil until they came for your body,
ready for that coffin, closely covered in black cloth.

Your days are finished.   All gone.
*No more shall we know you.**

But they speak of your smile.
How you lit up someone's day;
How you lit up the room.

(2007)

Here is my second prompt:

There is a sliding semi-circular concertina door to pull across the opening and it has never been pulled across.

Here I am open to all the elements. On my own. I suppose if it gets cold, or the rain comes in, I will have to close this door across the opening. Here I may choose to live close to the natural elements. At last I am free. With sea, wind, sky, light. This is what I want. People may visit, sit in my room. There is no furniture. Only carpet.

I sleep on rugs. Rugs to cover for warmth. I sit on rugs. Softly woven rugs, coarse rugs, plain rugs, patterned rugs.

Now I am parent-less. I will have visitors here, but not my parents. They are no longer able to come because they are dead. But I may visit them in their house up the road because I am alive. They have to stay in the house for the dead. That is a rule for the dead.

And I have a concertina door to pull closed whenever I want and against what I do not want. People do not come in by this door. They have a door for humans. The concertina door is the one I shut and open at will. No human comes in that way. It is there for me alone. Through that door I have the light, the sunrise and the sunset, the night sky and the stars. That is my door and I need no names for anything. Because this is the door leading out of language into experience.

As I wrote that last paragraph, I also thought this is the door through which I, and only I, will go also to my dying. That is why it is only for me and has never been closed yet. This was a particular feeling I remembered at the time my father died. In this poem about my father's death, the repetitions of 'you' are not about my father but about myself. In the second stanza the 'you' refers to how I reinvented my life every time I survived a serious mental illness.*

Spiralled Lives

a poem for inner voices
with lines from *Lament for Ignacio Sanchez Mejias*
by Federico Garcia Lorca*

There was a reason, you see
for thinking of death every day.
          You are here at its edge
     where you are dying
               and dying and dying.

So many times you have died I've lost count.
Your lives have been shed, stored in spirals somewhere.
Yet you are all the lives you ever lived.
Yes, it's for real this time.   This is the easy one.

You saw it when he died,
you knew as death was coming at five o'clock
It was exactly five in the afternoon
You knew one day it would be your turn.

Now
     Soon
          Certainly.

And will I miss the moment?
He died at five o'clock
at five in the afternoon.

What will the time be for me?

(2001)

It is an exacting moment sitting by the bed-side of the first parent who dies. The concertina door gave me the insight that it was within my power to open and close it against the elements, but when I die I will have no choice and go through for the last time to the vast unknown. However much older I become, and however much (at times) I lose the fear of dying, this transition (that we can never truly know) returns with traces of fearfulness in odd moments.

Physical death is the only experience in life we are sure not to have until the end, and then I will not be able to write about it at all. That frightens me because with all experiences in life, I have been able to write about them.

But I will not be able to write about dying as I die. I will only be able to live my death. And then I will be dead. And then I will no longer be here. These thoughts came to me often after both my parents died. They scared me. It was, and still is, difficult to conceive of not being alive, particularly when there is so much to live for and experience in life.

MEANING UNCOVERED THROUGH WRITING

This dream writing was emotionally charged as I engaged with the unfolding of the process. It uncovered layers of meaning about my own existence. My physical and emotional separation from my parents was obvious immediately. But the dream brought *home* to me my separate emotional self, my very different values, the very different way I live my life. And the word *home*, used abstractly here, is about inhabiting a separate *home* to my parents in this dream.*

This sea house was startlingly new as a space for me alone. Yet in the dream I knew I could and would visit my parents so I was not cutting myself off from their memory within me. But it was crucial they were absent and could not visit the sea house which was mine alone.

Writing about my long sea house allowed me to define, consolidate, and truly know my separate existence from my parents. Never mind that they were no longer in the physical world to visit me, or me them. Perhaps I had to wait for their deaths before I could ever feel that quality of separation. So much responsibility was laid on my shoulders whilst they were alive. Sometimes only with the death of a parent can we experience becoming fully adult in our own right.

As I suspected the dream itself was on an experiential level. I have to admit it might have been enough to have had the dream experience without exploration through writing. A thousand or so words told me what I already knew, but maybe could not have articulated so lucidly.

And having diaries going back many years means that in 2018 I could pinpoint the exact day I had that dream. It took a bit of detective work. I was in Yorkshire and the date was 26 April 2010, headed *Amazing Dream* with a little diagram of the juxtaposition of my annexe house and the main house. I find that curiously satisfying. It happened. I recorded it. And now I can refer back to the immediacy of the original writing. I also remember swathes of daffodils because I noted that too: the descendants of Wordsworth's daffodils were everywhere I drove in Yorkshire, all the way to the Lake District in the North of England.

I record a lot of dreams and have many vivid ones. This one lives on. That is because I wrote about it and that process fixes it in my mind as significant. Sometimes I find the point is to tell the dream only, sometimes to write it up only, and sometimes not to bother at all. Only by writing do I uncover these richly layered truths. Even though I have done this sort of writing over many years, I never take this for granted, nor anticipate. Conversations indeed give insights, but I find writing goes in more creative directions.

And I can read them back to myself. They become a permanent reminder of what was expressed at the time.

The natural world of the sea with its fluidity and potential for different temperaments and moods symbolizes the enormity of an oceanic inner life. The potential for writing so much more was implicit in the dream. I choose what I wanted to explore. I set limits. I set my own boundaries.

The next chapter explores those boundaries which are fixed in many different ways; some where form and shape do not exist at all, and how creative and therapeutic writing enables the shifting of inner emotional boundaries.

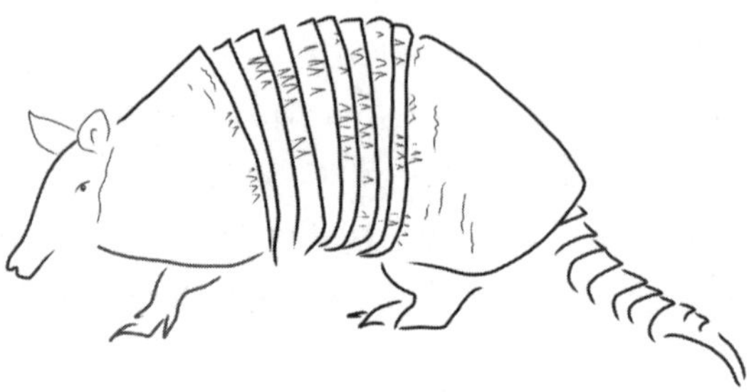

Writing To Do

Dream Snatch

- Choose just one image or a vivid sequence
- Re-write in the present tense to bring the scene to life
- Allow your feelings to surface and include in your writing
- Allow the writing itself to become an experiential process

Dream House

- Choose a house / room which appears in your dreams
- Or a house from your childhood or early life
- Describe everything you see as clearly as possible
- Walk around the house / room and note your feelings
- Note also if anyone else is there
- Go with any changes of details that occur as you write
- Describe your relationship to this house
- Write about what this house means to you

Writing To Do

On Separation

My parents moved to my childhood home when I was two years old: a solidly built 1920s house, a hundred yards from the sea. It featured in my life for the next fifty years, until my father died. As teenagers, my sister and I called our mother and father collectively *The Parents* which created a sense of us and them. The dream in this chapter was about my felt experience of real physical and emotional separation from them.

Whether dead or alive, write about the type of connection you have to:

- Mother / Mum / however you call her
- Father / Dad / however you call him

Write about your own experience as an individual and separate human being to:

- Mother / Mum / however you call her
- Father / Dad / however you call him

On a Grandparent

Write about a favourite grandparent and their home which perhaps you stayed in as a child. Include the feeling of connection with them.

- Describe the grandparent
- Describe the bedroom you slept in
- Describe your favourite meal
- Describe the journey there from your own home
- Describe an event which happened there
- Describe another event which happened there

Writing from Puns & Prompts

Puns & Meanings of Words

Some words sound the same but have different meanings and spellings; many words have more than one meaning. *Hold*, for example, is a noun for a storage place on a ship or aeroplane. *To hold* is a verb – physical as in *holding hands*, or abstract to hold someone to a promise or to *hold* energy as further down the page. *Holed up* sounds similar, means something else. I could have done more exploration with the word *concertina* describing the semi-circular door at the end of the dream sea-house. Or with the meaning of my dream coming *home* to me. I did, however, play with the word *cross.*

In my dream snatch, the word *cross-road*
became a prompt for writing about the feeling of anger
towards and from my parents

Explore and play with the words that appear in your writing.

Read through your writing. Underline any sentences or phrases that jump out at you. These are the sentences which *hold* the energy for more exploration and then become your prompts. Choose one at a time from which to freewrite.* And pick out words that have more than one meaning.

Choose your prompt

- Write the phrase or sentence down on a fresh page
- Rewrite: change tenses if you feel like it
- Choose a time limit of 6, 10 or 20 minutes
- Write freely and flow with whatever comes

Repeat this process

- Underline any phrase or sentence in the new piece that jumps out at you
- Write it down on a fresh page
- Rewrite: change tenses if you feel like it
- Choose your time limit
- Write freely and flow with whatever comes

Repeat as many times as the content of your writing energizes you and your interest. Write until you are satisfied. Do this over a few days or weeks, rather than all at once.

On Writing, Just Writing

In every room in my house, there is a pad of paper (usually yellow with lines) and pencils. I feel very odd if I am not in reach of paper and pencil wherever I am. Because ideas come as I move around, come out of the shower, chop onions in the kitchen. I need to be able to scribble notes down. And accumulate the sacred backs of envelopes with my notes for later. Sitting in cafés with my A5 notebook as I wait, I may be writing anything at all. As long as I'm writing. Just like Abigail Thomas in her book, *Thinking About Memoir.*

A diary isn't sacred . . . Call it a diary – it is less imposing than a journal . . . I am addicted. I need to feel my hand scribbling across a page. A friend [in a café] wanted to know what I was working on . . . and leaned over and read, 'It is taking a long time to get my sandwich.'
(Thomas 2008, pp.12/13 adapted)

On Dream Writing

In the inner world, the truth is that we not only have to be released from our parents we also have to learn to release them.
(Faraday,1972, p.241)

Finding meaning through dream writing owes much to advances after Freud's interpretative dream analysis to *the royal road of the unconscious.* The integration of personality in the 'here and now' through dream work, rather than tracing back to some neurotic trauma from the past, was the work of Dr Fritz Perls.* Gestalt therapy originated with him and at the time of his death in 1970, a young psychologist, Dr Ann Faraday* was starting her own post-graduate studies on dreams. In *Dream Power*, she explores the gestalt approach. My own dream writing owes much to gestalt therapy groups which I took part in during the seventies.

Redraft & Edit

Later take your pieces of writing, read through them slowly. Redraft your scribblings into a few paragraphs that please you. Give your writing a title and date it. A good idea when you look back at your writing. Time is deceptive. Do this over a few days or weeks. When you are ready, check your piece for sentence construction and spellings. Have you been clear in what you have written? Read to trusted others and ask for feedback, if that's what you'd like. Continue to redraft and edit your piece. That's the final stage.

CHAPTER 2

Shifting Boundaries

It is tempting to think about the permanence of boundaries as defined in the dictionary:

Boundary

A thing which serves to mark the limits of something, a dividing line

(OED)

A cluster of trees used as a boundary

(Old Breton)

But my writing about boundaries has widened this narrow scope and explored a shifting nature. Travelling around and noticing boundaries, like *clusters of trees* or walls and fences, has made me see more clearly the edges of things. But observational writing also invited descriptions of eroding sea cliffs and the aurora in the Arctic sky. Neither are static.

My process of writing has made me reassess the nature of *boundaries.* As I grasped the significance of an expanded concept, I have become far more aware of multi-nuanced ideas. Over a life-time I can now appreciate how my own personal boundaries have changed and transformed. Conversely I thought about where no boundaries exist at all in our universe. Even with scanty knowledge, in order to write I must understand the broad definition of paradigms like space-time and infinity. I learn through my writing and in this chapter I have done my best to stretch the limits of my understanding and shift the boundaries of my comprehension.

THE ULTIMATE BOUNDARY

The concertina wall at the end of my dream sea-room in the last chapter made me face my own eventual death, as did the death of my father. When a parent in their eighties dies this may be anticipated, but the dying of a friend of about my age brought much sadness and grief after the shock of a cancer diagnosis.

Sally and I met in London whilst our children were toddlers. As well as family life, we shared a common interest in writing and journalism. Our friendship continued as the children grew up into their twenties. It was then that Sally received her cancer diagnosis. Until the illness took hold, she fully embraced her life and then there was a transition into a state of grace with which she accepted her dying.

This is an extract from the last piece she wrote on staying in the hospice. Apparently she was even planning some corrections on the day she died.

> The poet Dylan Thomas said we should *Rage, rage against the dying of the light.** I would rather feel I were being pushed out in a boat into a calm sea. Here [in the hospice] I feel that calm, also airiness, quiet attention. Doctors, nurses, physios, cleaners, cooks, volunteers all convey a sense of unhurried attention. This calms, removes anxiety which in turn reduces pain. Pain takes away yourself. It sends you into a deep hole that you can not climb out of. Relief from pain brings you back to yourself.
>
> So calm, peace, space to reflect: these are what the hospice has given me. So yes, a place where people go to die but gratitude, not rage, is the boat I would like to go out on.
>
> (Sally Tolputt, June 2013)

There was no doubt that Sally felt peace in the hospice; I had experienced and shared that with her on my last visit. We both rested for about an hour as I reclined on the visitor's armchair alongside her bed. One of the nurses came in and said, *it is so peaceful in here*. It brought comfort to me and to all who knew her that *gratitude was the boat* Sally went in as she crossed the threshold of her life into the unknown realm of death.

THE BOUNDARIES OF DECISION MAKING

Before her diagnosis, Sally had been wondering whether to move house or not. This was a real dilemma and I made a suggestion for her to try and solve the decision through a writing exercise. I suggested it might be helpful to hand over some of her thinking to an *Internal Decision Maker*. Bringing such a person to mind who might be good at making decisions can be instructive. I asked her to imagine someone, historical or contemporary, who she thought was good at making decisions.

She came up with the great idea of King Solomon* fulfilling this role. *Brilliant* I thought. An inner wise-self as decision-maker. Her task, I mooted, was to write a dramatic dialogue between herself and King Solomon about whether to move house or not. Since she loved the theatre, I thought this would appeal but she did not follow it up. I wondered what King Solomon might have said about this kind of dilemma and so I set to with my own version of an imaginary dialogue:

Indecisive Self

I have a decision I don't know how to think about at the moment. I am not ready to make it. Everyone is telling me it is my decision, and either way it is fine. A decision one way or another has to be made but there is no immediate urgency to make it. Only I am unsure if it is a good idea to do one thing or a bad idea to do the other. Everyone has said they will go along with my decision and it does affect the whole family. I am so unsure that I don't even know what I want. I can't even say: *No, I don't want that or Yes, I do want this.*

King Solomon The Decision Maker

If you do not make a decision, events and time will play themselves out. If you cannot make a decision, don't make it. Life in the end will make it for you.

King Solomon's wisdom was praised in the bible. An imaginary dialogue with another historical figure might fit the bill equally well; or a charismatic person from contemporary life. A person known or someone in the public eye.

I know from my own experience that it is good when I recognize that I am not always in the right place to make a decision. When the time is right and I finally come to a decision, there is invariably relief. I may not have been aware how much of a burden I had been carrying. A solution when reached gives boundaries to the dilemma, whatever it might be, packages it up and sorts it out. And life carries on.

Except for Sally, life only carried on for another two years. None of us, Sally included, had any idea that Life (capital L) was going to make a far more serious decision for her. This meant that staying in the home she knew was certainly best, near to friends and familiarity. In a prescient way, without knowing why, perhaps this underlaid her uncertainty. Within days of a visit to the doctor, and an immediate hospital consultation, Sally crossed the boundary of perceived health into the diagnosis of cancer and into that country of illness.*

(For a series of haiku texts I sent to her in the hospice, see page 90.)

MY PERSONAL BOUNDARIES

The first time I crossed the border into the country of illness was in my early twenties when mental illness blasted apart any sense of personal boundaries. There is no privacy in a psychiatric hospital ward and chronic depression took away any sense of self whatsoever. I am lucky, however, that my illnesses were self-limiting, bounded by a beginning which came upon me over three days, and after months and months or even twelve of them, spiralled me into wellbeing over a matter of days equally quickly. Here I crossed the boundaries: stepped over the threshold of wellness into illness, and back to health again.

Writing the first book in this series about my clinical depression, *A Fox Crossed My Path*, shifted my feelings of shame and secrecy in the current climate of a more open society in the twenty first century. Over my life-time I have experienced this shifting of the taboo around mental illness.

RULES MAKE BOUNDARIES

In my many years of being well, I held onto an assumption that I had broken away from a rule-bound upbringing which had restricted a natural maturing as an adolescent. In my mid-twenties I rebelled and became a freer spirit with hippy values. In the era after the swinging sixties, I thought having no boundaries was a good thing. The prim parents' rules were transcended with a sexual freedom I found wildly liberating. Sex was fun, that is not what I had been led to believe.

My upbringing in a middle-class and not particularly religious, but socially observant Jewish family celebrated the important festivals. In peace-time after the horrors of World War Two, family circumstances meant I grew up in a sea-side town away from the North London Jewish community where my grandparents lived and my own parents grew up, and which later I felt was my natural home.

There are many rules in Judaism*, particularly rules about restricted food eg: no ham or pork at home, but those about shellfish were broken when convenient because when we went out to a restaurant, we always had a prawn cocktail.

There were unwritten rules too such as the value of money and which friendships were suitable. And one implicit and unwritten rule growing up in a non-Jewish community, about boys: it was pretty clear, there would be no suitable boys where we lived. That did not make it hard to follow another overt rule: no sex before marriage.

As an adolescent, these bounded rules dominated my life although I knew nothing different. So I would never have thought of them as boundary-making. Only through writing about my upbringing, have I come to the realization these were in fact the boundaries that my parents instilled in me.

Years of living as an independent adult finding my own boundaries has given me enormous freedom from what might have been a restricted and more conventionally led life. In my dream of the long sea house, it was significant that this was my separate living place from *the parents*. My unconscious dream life made my own separate boundaries obvious. Yet in the dream I could visit *the parents* in their new house for the dead. When they were alive, I struggled with a lack of clear boundaries between us.

Writing about my upbringing, the sea room and my own personal boundaries shows me how much I have achieved. Even if it has taken most of my life to feel a separate and independent being in my own right, and shift those rigid boundaries belonging to a different generation.

In the following piece, I establish how my personal boundaries are strongly in place:

My own boundary is rooted in the sense of myself as a person: to do with my time, particularly in my house and my personal space. And my person. Not only the skin around me but the field of energy around me too. I am sensitive to how close someone is to me. If I am drawn to another person then being close is a shared intimacy, maybe only for a moment or two. If I am averse to someone, and I may not even be able to name what that is, I move away. My invisible boundary stretches to the things I am willing to do for others and the limit of what I am willing to put up with when feeling over-stretched. When I need to say No that tells me my boundary of giving stops there.

(My Notes, 2011)

Here a respectful awareness of boundaries between me and other people is demonstrated as well as knowing what I need for my own sense of wellbeing. I find my self-imposed rules give me the guidelines for both *Yeses* and *Nos* in my life. In practical terms, I will limit myself to just one television programme in an evening, say *Yes* to one, maybe two glasses of wine. I will find a kind way of saying *NO* to that person who may have stepped over my personal boundary. These decisions define my idea of boundaries which of course shift around depending on circumstances, the tasks in hand and my levels of energy.

Yet whilst I was exploring this issue of boundaries in my late sixties, I wrote something which stopped me in my tracks. Because I recognzed its truth mirroring my original premiss of having no boundaries at all. This assumption had been scuppered by all the exploratory writing I did. But here it was again:

In my personal writing I have no boundaries, which is why I need to do it.

What did I mean? I went on to ask myself these questions:

> What does having no boundaries in my personal writing give me? Why do I need to write?

Here is the relevant extract:

> It answers the creative source inside me. Creativity bubbles up, whether from within or without, when I am feeling open in mind and feelings. I am truly creative when I am receptive to what wants to come into and through my writing without form.
>
> (My Notes, 2011)

Here was an insight I welcomed, finding out that the initial creative splurges came from a boundary-less place within myself. I knew such a place existed in myself and my writing confirmed this. Here was where my earlier assumption about not wanting boundaries had migrated, shifted even. So through my writing I discovered that my boundaries were secure in everyday life, and transcended in my creative life. That distinction makes me very happy. I am after all, at times, a free spirit shifting my own boundaries within the safety of my own writing process.

BREAKING BOUNDARIES WITH A STRANGER

We teach our children how to keep safe, not to talk to strangers because of the potential of inappropriate behaviour transcending their own personal boundaries. But I am often exchanging a few words in passing with people I'll never see again, particularly when I visit London. Here is a brief memory, that if I had not written it down, would have been lost in the mists of my mind.

This piece was probably written up from notes jotted down in my A5 Notebook. I wrote in the third person, although the person is clearly me:

> An older woman sees a free space on a bench in the courtyard of a grand historic house in London. On the bench is a young man smoking a cigarette. He thoughtfully blows the smoke away from the woman as he sees she is eating a sandwich. They sit in silence. He smoking; she eating. The light is going. It is March and at last after days of never ending rain, the weather is dry, warmer.
>
> He breaks the silence, talks to her about the courtyard, but more about the sky above. She hadn't been paying attention whilst enjoying her sandwich. As the light is going the clouds are highlighted grey and shaped. They sit in silence and look. The clouds become dramatic, fuller, making the whole sky as if a canvas. She says: *Thank you for making me look*. He says: *I would have liked to sit here when they had finished building and seen it then*. He tells her he has just got a job in London in an architect's office. His soft lilt tells her he is Irish. *No jobs there, he says. Everything is happening in London.*
>
> (My Notes, 2014)

As strangers we shared our common humanity through conversation. The young man broke the boundary of silence and I thought our brief meeting memorable enough to write about. Noting boundaries was uppermost in my mind at this time and I was seeing them everywhere. Here boundaries are clear or implicit in almost every sentence: highlighting the material world as well as the person-to-person interaction; the boundaries of the courtyard were formed with Georgian facades on three sides of a square; the woman was in a separate gender and age category from the young architect; the bench was made of planks of wood separating air from matter to allow sitting, and the grey-white clouds were outlined against a darkening blue sky with each colour bounded from the other until the darkness blurred all edges.

Looking at the sky and talking about the atmosphere of the courtyard provided a congenial connection and the conversation lasted less than fifteen minutes, a quarter of an hour. Something I noted, being time-conscious.

THE BOUNDARY OF TIME

We measure the flow of time with twelves and sixties, hours and minutes which are universally recognized with clocks and sophisticated time-keepers marking out and separating our days.* Our perception of time is dependent on this sequence of numbering which gives us a form of boundary as one minute shifts to the next.

The flow of time goes on and on, and as I stop to write about it, I know I find the far distant future hard to think about. This leads me then to think about the concept of infinity. *Mathematics cannot really handle infinite numbers*, wrote Stephen Hawking* in *A Brief History of Time* (Hawking 1988, p.46). Although the symbol ∞ for infinity is clearly defined with a horizontal twisted figure of eight loop which has no beginning or end.

No-one knows about conceptual time before the Big Bang.* The universe we live in appears to be without boundaries. And in some unimaginable future all that we have in our galaxy may collapse, shrink back and disappear into a black hole.* As if nothing that is, ever was.

Complex and evolving theories about space, time and the universe are beyond me, but writing these few sentences stretches my internal imaginative boundaries of ideas. Inevitably I will fail on the science, but superficial knowledge has to be good enough, and that in itself is sufficiently satisfying to stretch my thinking through writing.

Coming closer to our own portion of the universe, I found a little more manageable. In this description, I note that nothing stays still. Everything is constantly shifting:

> Everything under the sun is on the move. The earth orbits on itself and around this massive ball of exploding gases held in shape through the force of gravity. The air in the atmosphere moves through our bodies as millions of cells inside us are constantly replacing themselves.
>
> (My Notes, 2012)

BODIES ARE SOFTLY BOUNDED

Although the cells inside my body may be renewing themselves continuously, my awareness rests around the boundary of my own skin. The outer layer of our physiological being gives us our body shape, one which is recognizable from a distance. I remember walking across a beach in Norfolk to join family one summer and though the sands were crowded with tourists, I spotted my relatives' physical contours from a distance long before I could see their faces.

My instructions had been to find Beach Hut 114. The sequential counting of numbers just using the numerals 0 – 9 is our ingenious method of identification, originally based on finger counting. There was a long row of similar huts. I just had to find the correct number.

> ### Beach Hut 114
>
> It is a small wooden structure on stilts with steps up to a veranda and a bench in the interior. I have known beach huts on promenades anchored to concrete plinths because during

stormy weather the waves will batter them to smithereens if they are not boarded up with steel cladding, padlocks and tethered down in the winter.

(My Notes, 2017)

Beach hut 114 is, at least for the moment, static and stable on an expanse of flat sands. The cliffs, however, in other parts of the county are vulnerable to erosion.

Norfolk Boundaries

The cliff edges erode, tumble down into the sea and change shape. Alter boundaries with newly formed cliff faces; fossils are revealed from thousands of years ago, and bricks from ruined houses are wedged into mud and grass tussocks. The geographical contours change by the year.

(My Notes, 2017)

There is nothing static or stable about those rugged sea cliffs. Painting a word picture in my mind brings back the colours of soil and sand, the shrubby coastal foliage and the feel of the wind whipping up the waves. I have this scene in my mind's eye through descriptive and observational writing. Perhaps that is because I have a visual mind, quickly able to conjure up images. That also helps if I want to add details to my writing, once home and at my desk.

Observational writing sharpens my awareness of the different qualities of the edges of things whether the shifting landscape of cliffs tumbling down, beach huts kept secure, or the way the human form is softly bounded. These descriptions have honed how I apply this versatile concept of boundaries.

The simple structure of a hut brought up memories of walking along the promenade in the sea-side town where I grew up, remembering the power of the sea lashing over the sea defences of concrete walls. Whilst writing, memories may always surface, breaking through the barriers in the mind and are worthwhile capturing as they emerge.

HOLIDAY WRITING

It is always a good idea to write as events happen, particularly on holiday. The writing then contains the freshness of the first impression, which can never be recreated later.

One November, I travelled on a large working and leisure ship along the Norwegian coast. As soon as we were on board, I set myself up in my cabin rather than go exploring this big floating ship. This is what I always do when away from home to make myself comfortable. Of course I had a number on the door for my own personal and private space:

Cabin 451

I am recreating my own boundaries, making them familiar in the unfamiliar environment on board a huge ship in foreign seas. I am in a cosy corner writing. Looking out of the window, the coast-line is dotted with lights. Door closed to the long corridor, no contact with fellow passengers. I have what I need: sleeping area; clothes in cupboards, books and things on shelves. And most importantly, a writing area by the porthole.

Once I had my pencil case, notebooks and a round brass tray (I always travel with) for my rubber and sharpener visible on a shelf, I had made the space my own and felt secure. I had been warned that at this time of year the skies might be dark for most of the time, that there would be barely any discernible boundary between day and night. This made me itch to write about the boundaries between dark and light.

BLURRED BOUNDARIES IN THE ARCTIC CIRCLE

There was much that I anticipated writing about on this trip. I had planned to pay particular attention to the geographical boundaries, and I thought I would be writing about the jagged edges of fjord shores. But from the ship's deck, I could barely see them. Nothing could really have prepared me for the very few hours of light, and the continuous grey blur of the coast-line.

As we approached the Arctic Circle, there was mounting excitement on board. Here are entries from my holiday notebook:

7.15 am: The cabin telephone announces in several languages we will cross the Arctic Circle in 15 minutes. And to note the marker bobbing on the sea's surface on the starboard side. But my cabin's window is on the port side. Through the window, it is dark. No going on deck. No sighting.

The Shifts Between Light and Dark

8.00 am: Dawn is slow. The sky is blue. The sea is ink dark.

11.00 am: Deck 6

We steer our path past a small bleak island. Barren islands, glacial rocks and outcrops. Grey clouds. Grey sky. A small oval of light, at edges of overlapping clouds. This is probably as light as it will get today.

13.40 pm: Deck 9

Dusk will be within the hour. Overcast, the sky is dull grey. It is twilight. Not very light. Not very dark. Cloud and sleet blur the boundaries between sky and sea. Mountains and villages are blurred outlines. All is grey. Except for electric lights in the windows, in the town, in the harbour. White houses picked out in light reflected, reversed on the water.

Late Evening: Deck 9 Northern Lights*
A fierce wind and chill. The boat tipping in the Barent Sea. No colour in the aurora: an arc around the dome of the sky. To the naked eye, the sky lightened and swirls of paler shades of greys and whites moved around.

Recording this new experience of the unrelenting lack of light in those few hours made me even more aware of our dependence on the sun. It made me realise how I take its daily appearance for granted. What little we saw of the Northern Lights put me in touch with a biblical feeling of awe about the power and vastness of the sky. It brought to mind ancient civilizations who worshipped the sun with its mysterious appearance and disappearance each day, and the many gods of the skies, even though my knowledge is scanty.

This observational writing later took me into a reflective space but I caught the moments as they happened. I always write the time down so a building up of the whole is achieved by the end of the day.

LANGUAGE AND THE BOUNDARY OF WORDS

The alphabet of 26 letters creates thousands of words
Language is a living changing entity
Over time

Whether I am writing from observation or ideas which have floated into my mind, the language (conceptual or concrete) is bounded through words. I build up my sentences into sequences, then into paragraphs. The use of punctuation brings an ordered sense of boundary and meaning firstly to myself, and then to you the reader.

Through writing I firm up my thinking with more precision. If it is a flimsy idea in the first place and the writing dries up, then

I discard that thought. It is really within my process of writing I find out if I have something to explore and articulate.

SPACES GIVE BOUNDARIES

Boundaries in writing invite space on the page to be acknowledged. The shape of letters and the space either side of a word is integral. The word then becomes positioned in its own (usually white) space; a boundary is given to allow for understanding. Although we may barely notice it.

Look at these sentences:

A black rat ran across the road.
A rat ran back across the road.
That road is a rat-run for cars.

Our brains are geared to make sense of words and meaning in the order they appear. This arrangement of words, separated one from the other, gives me quite different information.

As soon as words are written down, I see the shapes of lines and curves on the white space of the paper. This allows my eye-brain co-ordination to know what each word signifies. Language and how the brain works is an enormous subject. Not within the scope of a book like this.

Nevertheless I can still make out the merging of letters as these words are run together, but it is harder work. I would find it easier if the words had their respective spaces:

Howevernotessentialyoucanstillmakeoutthissentence
wherethewordsruntogether

And if I listen to a language different from my own, I may not distinguish separate words, although I will be alert to the sounds to try and decipher their specific identity. If I am say in the sitting area of my grown-up children's house and they are speaking in low tones in the kitchen space (no boundary walls, all is open plan) I am also unable to distinguish the separate words.

CREATIVE WORDS: BEYOND BOUNDARIES

Getting the words down on paper in written form acts as a catalyst to creativity. Creativity, as I wrote previously, *bubbles up* and may go beyond the boundaries of what I know. And then suddenly those boundaries dissolve and I find myself in uncharted territory. This can be exciting or it may be scary. Finding the words to express and say what is going on from that blurry place reinstates a boundary with definition, and I can then find my way back to reference points and familiarity.

MIND MAPS*

The regularity of creating a mind map each morning
keeps me grounded and well bounded
with a visual guide for the structure of my time

My tasks, my activities, and most importantly my meals go onto my mind map on a clean side of scrap paper (always A4 size). This stays on the kitchen table all day and helps me prioritize the important things to do. It is better than a list. But here is a list of the benefits:

* I clear my mind from clutter with this focus.
* I do not give myself a hard time about what I do not achieve.
* Some achievable goals are always reached by bed-time.

The next morning I transfer what has not been achieved onto a fresh mind map and shred the mind map of the previous day.

THE BOUNDARY OF MY DIARY

In my diary, I clarify and process my feelings. It encloses me in privacy within the hard cover of its binding. Instead of allowing a continual whirring around in my mind and body of thoughts and feelings I give them the boundaries provided by writing. Often I write about minor discomforts and reflections on the previous day. I can then start the day with a clear mind. Of course, bigger issues may need more extensive writing or discussion with a trusted other.

The last piece in this chapter comes from a diary-write and uses metaphor to try and make sense of a relationship (see the beginning of the next chapter for an explanation of metaphor). Insight through metaphor explodes into an understanding beyond the boundaries of logical thinking. Here is a perfect example of how this works, revealing a personal boundary operating an effective defence system. The writing was triggered from my own feelings of discomfort about another person.

Armadillo

Anne (not her real name) was behaving in a way which was beyond what I could make sense of, and I was feeling uncomfortable. I needed to understand her better and found myself puzzling about her own invisible boundary because I was beginning to feel disconnected in our conversations.

I started by asking myself to conjure up an image of Anne as an animal, or bird or type of fish. The image of an armadillo came to my mind in a flash:

> An armadillo is a solitary creature burrowing into the earth and lives alone in a burrow; usually found in South America. It has overlapping, leather-hard scales. The word itself comes from the Spanish word for armour. It is a great defence against predators and it also hides in prickly bushes to protect itself. But its underside is soft skin and fur so it can curl up into a ball.

Here is my freewrite after I thought of Anne as the armadillo:

> Her defence system is like an armadillo's and she deflects all criticism. Troubles run like water off her back. She wades into crises and comes out the other side unscathed. Her armadillo-like behaviour leads her into situations most people would avoid. She does this knowingly; loading the weight of others' troubles onto the thick hide of her back. Then she throws these off and scurries off to her burrow.

In the equivalent of her burrow, I guess Anne is able to be with her own vulnerability and solitary self. This writing gave me a different perspective and I stopped trying to work out what was motivating her behaviour. Now when I find myself thinking about her, the armadillo accompanies my thoughts.

Writing about the armadillo gave me a precise image of how this boundary operated and hid vulnerability. Although all my questions were not answered, this writing proved helpful, and I had answered my primary question about Anne's boundary and felt more comfortable. My own perception, of course, is mine alone and I did not share this.

The writing in this chapter has shifted around all kinds of boundaries: fixed and unfixed, invisible and non-existent, of language and numbers, of life and death. As well as about spaces around the boundary of words on the page and an exploration about my own inner space and the source of creativity. I have come to the realization through this writing that my life is indeed well-bounded and grounded in my sense of self: both in my physical body and within the walls of my house.

Writing has the power to shift difficult feelings. When I enter my imagination through engaging with metaphor as I did about Anne, I may get a glimpse of *the other* more clearly. I unlock writing that tells me something my rational mind does not know. There is a release of power which gives me far more understanding about my friendships and the opportunity to make my connections more authentic.

In the next chapter, I extend this exploration of metaphor and show how I have crossed the boundaries from the reality of my day-to-day relationships into the inner life of the imagination.

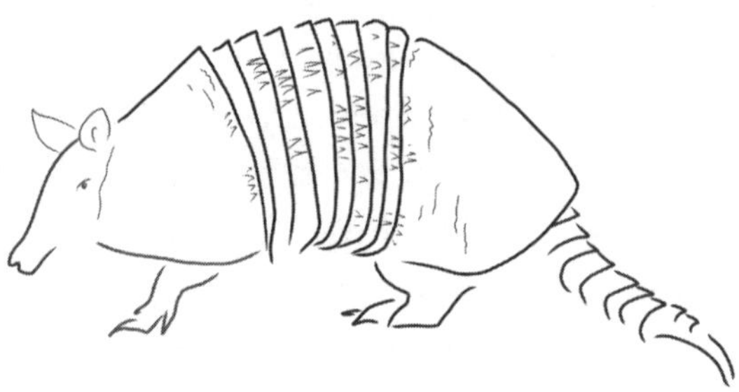

Writing To Do

The Internal Decision Maker

Handing over to an internal character of your own choosing may help you find a solution your conscious brain is failing to solve.

- Imagine someone you admire from history or contemporary life
- Write a dialogue between yourself and your internal decision maker about the decision

Try This

- Draw a line vertically down a blank piece of paper
- Write Pros one side, Cons the other side
- List everything you can think of on one side and the other
- Do this quickly and randomly
- Evaluate the length of your lists – is the decision obvious?

If no conclusion is reached

- Extend your dialogue over several days
- Write about not being able to make a decision
- Reflect on all that you have written

Writing To Do

Your Own Personal Boundaries

The suggestions below might benefit from frequent and short stints over a period of time: perhaps ten or twenty minutes each day for a week, or find your own rhythm.

- Freewrite on the boundaries (maybe think in terms of rules) which you received from your birth family eg: certain topics are never discussed

  (for an explanation about freewriting see p.43 and p.104)
- Write more on what might have been unwritten rules (boundaries)
- Describe the impact these implicit and obvious boundaries gave you when growing up
- Respond with an outline of how your sense of personal boundaries may have shifted as you grew up
- Pinpoint your awareness of boundaries now
- Note the shifts as you go about your daily life
- Jot down when you notice your boundaries shift around
- Scribble about static boundaries; those which won't budge

Writing To Do

When the armadillo came to mind as a metaphor for a friend, I knew nothing about it as a creature. Clearly my imagination had a keen sense of what fitted. I may think I know my friends but this was a metaphor which taught me that's not always the case. We learn about ourselves and others all the time. And this writing with metaphor helps the process amazingly.

Boundaries, Metaphor and The Self

Animals on the land, birds in the sky and fish in the sea are plentiful and give us so many images. Images which have the power to reflect ourselves and the quality of our boundaries. Some days these may be fixed; other times our boundaries shift according to circumstances and whose company we are in.

Freewrite:

- Describe a creature of the land, sea or air to reflect your mood NOW
- Describe the details which would make up your physical boundaries. If I was my cat I'd fluff up my fur to appear bigger, spread out my claws in readiness to scratch, grimace to reveal my sharp teeth and hiss before running for cover under a piece of furniture.
- Do this exercise another day when you are feeling in a different mood
- Imagine the metaphor for your creative self. Write about the quality of these boundaries. Remember my sense was that I had none (see p.25-6).

Think of a friend or relative you would like to understand better. Write as described in this chapter and above. Consider keeping your insights to yourself. In my close relationships, I use my judgement when to share and certainly keep my thoughts to myself when there is no advantage to speaking. I share only if the mood and circumstances feel right.

Holiday Writing

Before I had even climbed the ship's ramp, I had made notes to myself about how relevant I thought the trip up the Norwegian coast would be to writing about boundaries. I saw the fjords in my imagination. I imagined my cabin would be like a cell. Small but adequate.

- Anticipate with Notes any writing project away from home before the experience
- Focus the mind with Anticipatory Notes, this frees up the mind for further ideas
- See how they match up with reality when you write about the real experience
- Write about new experiences as soon as possible while you have first impressions
- Fill these out later when you have more information to add
- Describe how you make a holiday space with its different boundaries comfortable as a home away from home
- Describe what makes you uncomfortable about your physical boundaries when on holiday
- Observe and write about the new boundaries you come across

Freewriting

Scribbling: getting down your thoughts and feelings, unhindered by emotional boundaries, of what is and what is not acceptable to write. Going with a flow of words which come from your own fingers without allowing your mind to judge. Ignoring the inner critical voices in your head implanted there by teachers or parents that what you are writing is no good. It doesn't matter. You can write out these internalized voices too. And then respond.

Find out what you really want to say. This is your writing: raw, untrammelled by any boundaries whatsoever, full of feelings and thoughts. Your own. No-one need see.

Literary Styles & Boundaries

After the splurges of freewriting is the time to think about boundaries for your writing. Decide whether you want others to read your work. Intentions are the motivating factor here.

Once you start with sentences, paragraphs, and word-limits you are thinking boundaries. These also depend on the writing: there is prose for articles and essays, novels and non-fiction, and many forms of poetry on the page. Boundaries, boundaries, boundaries.

Redraft and luxuriate in redrafting to fully explore the content. The form of your writing may make itself clearer during this process. Then the editing process kicks in. Now is the time to check spellings and grammar, the look on the page, not forgetting those spaces. Consistency of voice and style. And knowing who your reader might be.

Contractions

In the main body of the book, I keep to the full use of separate words like I am, I have, or other words which informally are used with an apostrophe for a missing vowel. My friend Sally said she preferred not to contract them in writing as we do in speech. I honour her in that way, but use contracted phrases in extracts, direct speech and these boxes.

Mind Map

Key words highlight the themes about boundaries explored in this chapter

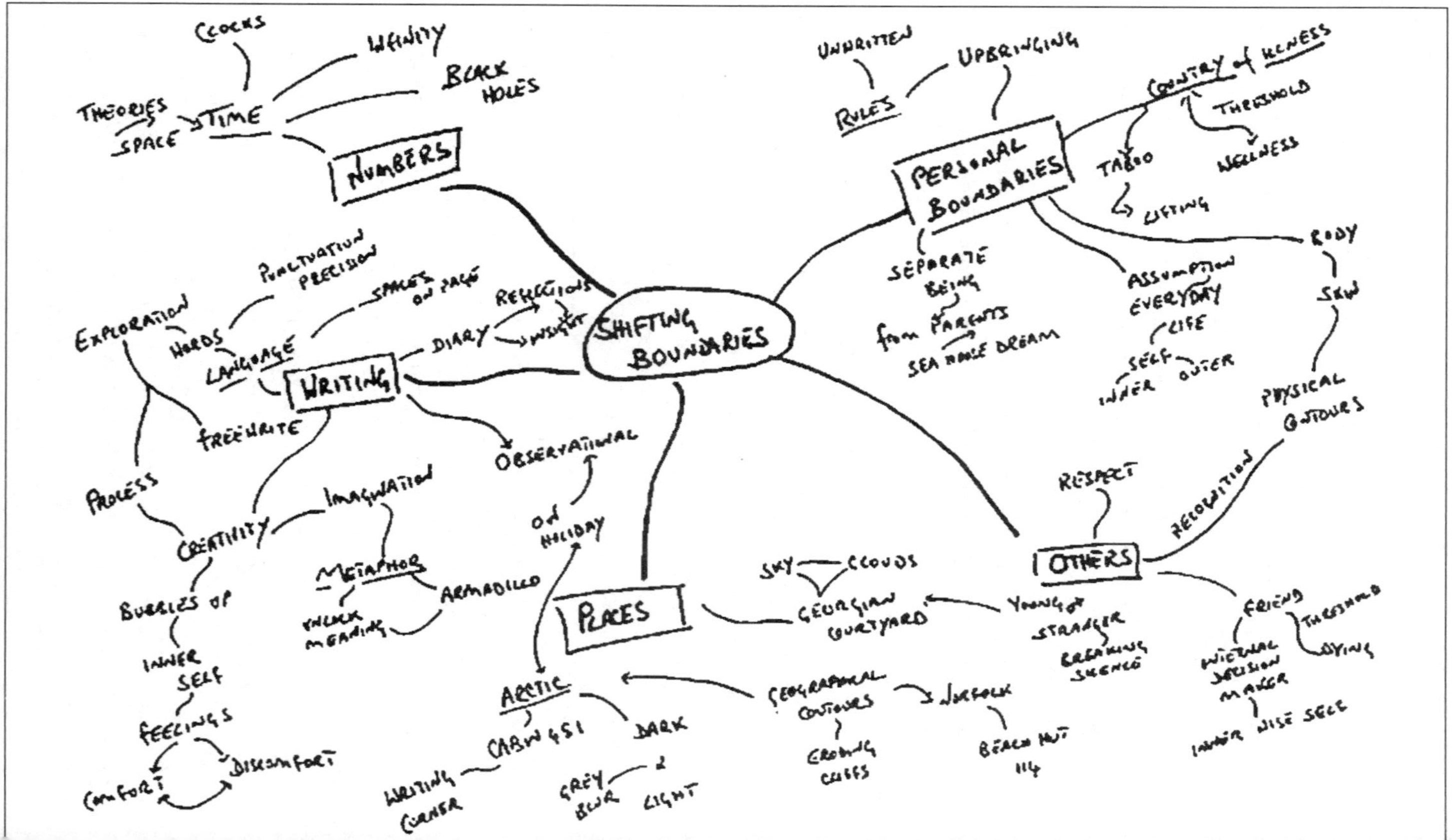

CHAPTER 3

Wall Fictions

In *Wall Fictions* I harness the imaginative richness of metaphor to look at my relationships. In the dramas of our inner lives, metaphor helps us understand our abstract feelings or states of being through transferring the abstract, and sometimes complex feelings, to something concrete we can visualize. Unlike similes which describe 'things' like 'something else', a metaphor transfers 'absolute meaning' to 'something else'. It does this quickly, providing immediate understanding, breaking through the boundaries of our literal thinking.

This exploration turned my walls into fictions and gave me insights to gauge the quality of my meetings with friends and family members. My walls became tangible and textured in my mind, offering condensed and potent meaning. This helped me see my relationships far more clearly. In this chapter I deal with the transformative power of writing to turn discomfort into insightful and manageable feelings. And I use visual language to explore safe and loving scenarios, which bring comfort to the inner self.

With spoken and written language, our direct communication with each other sometimes belies the non-verbal and unspoken. When I meet another person and form a rapport, my approach is much influenced by Martin Buber's philosophy of *I and Thou*.* His core belief pivots around how we live through relationship: 'You are brought into the fullness of your existence and become truly yourself only through the I-Thou relation' (Ravenscroft, 2017, p.36).

When I imagined two walls to symbolize myself and another, I became increasingly aware of the space between me and the other human being. This prompted me to wonder:

What is this space like?
How far away or close is it?

And so the exchange of energy between me and another involves an interplay of behaviour which is both conscious and subliminal. I might say between the boundaries of myself and the other person.

Stories from my childhood are always surfacing when I am writing. Perhaps more significant, however, is the writing from my own inner child. When writing from this perspective, I engage with a *Naïve Voice* because I never lose the knowledge I am an adult writing from the place of my inner child. This process feels naïve in the sense the word may be used in art for painters like Henri Rousseau.* I express myself in the simplest words with minimal punctuation. This expressive writing emphasizes simplicity with a child-like awareness, but the feelings revealed are serious, far from childish.

My childhood home remained a family house for fifty years. I was two years old when my parents settled there after World War Two had disrupted their own young adult lives. Understandably they sought security, but the well-built, spacious 1920s house felt suspended in time, emotionally blocked up like the no longer needed chimney places. The house became filled with antiques like a museum. Dust was not allowed to settle. The sea air did not permeate the walls, and there was no emotional fire. Although I am only able to describe it like this, as I think back. I may have had a functional security in the longevity of my birth family home, but as I grew up I did not find comfort there.

THEATRE OF THE MIND

The writing of this first story comforted me when everyday life was stressful. Here is a *wall fiction* which felt real in the theatre of my mind. I was in my mid-fifties creating an imaginative dwelling for my inner child; a place to feel safe and secure.

The dream writing about the long sea house gave me a wonderful imaginary space for my adult self to visit on her own. Here, I write about a different place: a small dwelling with rounded walls fit for my inner little girl, who has always had a sense of freedom and mischief.

This is a story about an igloo, a mud one. To write it, I thought like a little girl and one who naturally wanted a friend to play with. And so there are two little girls in the story.

At first I had no names for my two characters and felt a resistance to naming the girls. I knew I had to resolve my dilemma, so I thought of names which carried meaning from my own childhood. One of my preferred names I called myself as a child was Lisa, which sounded exotic to me. I named the other little girl after my best friend at school, Dottie. Once I inserted these names into the piece, it transformed. Immediately the characters felt rounded and real, like the little girls they were meant to be. Only at that stage did I feel that the writing became a proper story.

Using only lower case letters helped to write myself into the feeling of being a small child. I wanted to find a voice which would give the impression of a little girl, too small to use capital letters or full stops. Considering I was imagining myself at three years old, I do not think I would be writing at all. Phrases were short. A little girl could not use long sentences. One thought for each one; this made for a staccato pace, reflecting one thing after another.

the mud igloo

two little girls of three years old skip across puddles run over muddy land wearing wellington boots lisa wears red ones dottie a yellow pair after a while lisa and dottie reach a green hill here they stop by a river and a flat expanse of earth with bare hands they scoop up piles of mud and pat them into brick shapes like the wooden bricks they have at home like the bricks in the walls of their own houses these shapes they know well the two little girls make lots and lots of bricks they line them up in rows they find the sun dries them out in the afternoon they build a house

lisa says *we will build our house all perfect and round* the girls position the bricks in a circle this isn't easy we *must have a door we must have a hole at the top for smoke* dottie insists *we will have a fire at night-time yes* says lisa *my daddy always makes a fire when we camp*

when it is all built the shape is an igloo a mud igloo they collect twigs lying around and grasses from the river bank we need bigger branches dottie says with great authority lisa spots several *here's some let's drag them in*

lisa and dottie crawl inside and make a bed each in the curves of the wall they build up a pile of twigs and branches in the middle for the fire so far this is all good then they come up against a problem a serious one they are not sure how to light the fire they are not sure what they will have for supper *daddy always has a big box of matches* lisa says, *and I am not allowed to hold the box I'm not allowed to go to bed dirty* says dottie

in their short lives they have been washed many times they know about being clean dottie makes a sensible suggestion *we'll go and paddle in the river and scrape all*

> *this muddy stuff off* and that's what they do then they creep back to the mud igloo and lie down because they are very tired they have had such a busy day when they are comfy in their beds, they tell each other stories all about their lives all three years just before they fall asleep lisa says *this is my home now I am never going to go back home to my mummy and daddy ever again*
>
> (2005)

This writing brought about useful and surprising insights I do not think I would have found with my grown-up voice. I wrote in the present tense so the story stays in a timeless imaginative zone. It is written in the third person so I, as author, can visualize the setting and the two little girls. The writing itself was done intuitively; the insights only came later, as I reflected on the hidden meanings in my narrative.

My father never made a fire; we never camped, nor did we ever go for a walk in the surrounding countryside. Both my parents grew up with fireplaces in their bedrooms and no central heating. Fires reminded them of life before World War Two with sooty dust everywhere. For them fires were old-fashioned. And so the daddy in the story is really my husband. We went camping as a family in the wild and his fire-making is legendary.

This was my first attempt at thinking like a child whilst writing; it was great fun. Not far below my adult surface lurks my mischievous young self, ever at the ready to come forward. During the process of writing, I felt a connection forged itself in the present between my adult inner child and the real child that I once was. I felt there was more exploration to do, and used the last sentence as a prompt for further writing:

> . . . lisa says: *this is my home now I am never going to go back home to my mummy and daddy ever again.*

Quite true. By 2005, my father was dead, my mother in a nursing home nearby. The old family house long sold. I was pretty sure I would be unlikely to return to take a look from the garden gate. And in all the years since this writing, I have not returned. Having grown up in this house from the age of two, and being over fifty by the time of the sale, the rooms and contents are so vivid in my mind's eye, that it all comes up in a flash whenever I give it any thought.

Writing that sentence, however, with my child consciousness was potent. I have found a hand-written note in my files as follows:

> The mud igloo image is so apposite, I can hardly believe its potency. The thawing of deep inner time when I am in such a non-verbal place.

My diaries mention feeling suspended in a glacial time, a desire to stay in the mud igloo quietly and for a long time, how the red brown mud walls are warming, the fire is blazing and will never go out. Although I built it with another little girl, I write, *she has to go away and I have to be on my own.*

But there will be visitors, I add. This is reminiscent of the long sea room. My inner child needed to have a companion in the beginning to build the imaginary igloo, but I might reason both little girls are part of me. And as the process of writing unfolds, I move into a more integrated sense of self.

I knew that my inner work to make the little girls safe inside my own self had to be done on my own. And as an adult.

More notes were in the file:

> *Now she is really on her own. She is not frightened. She is not at all cross. She just cannot leave this place.*

Later I did more writing about *lying in the mud igloo* as an adult. *Weak, ill and dying.* Four friends arrive and sit at my head, feet and each side:

> *here something of her dies peacefully as she is watched over and something very gentle is coming to life for the first time ever.*

This writing was pivotal in making me realise how safety in the present could be provided imaginatively. I was never safe in that solidly built house of my childhood, where I felt suffocated and stifled at times during my growing up. At five years old, I even packed a suitcase to leave home (I have no idea where I found one I could carry). I was discovered outside the front gate on the pavement, as I was not allowed to cross the road.

Writing as an adult with this child perspective brought up contrasting feelings of detachment and a new sense of curiosity. What was I doing aged five, wanting to leave home? I have no idea. I don't remember what was happening at the time.

Easier to remember 2005. My days were long, busy and crowded. Too many people pulling me from all directions, as I was responsible for my mother in the nursing home and her affairs, still involved with school runs, and a family role at home. I had little time of my own, was scribbling and writing poems in snatches of time. I desperately needed a place to be alone. I probably got it in the car, and sometimes when I was lying in bed. Then I would think of the mud igloo and feel comforted.

The mud igloo story was a landmark in my imaginative writing. Solid and indestructible. I had built a safe home in my own mind. No-one could pull down lisa and dot's mud igloo. Because no-one could reach it. Because no-one knew where it was. My own impetuous and mischievous inner child found she had expressed herself in writing.

THE VALUE OF SCRIBBLING

Looking through other scraps of paper, I was surprised to find one dated August 2002. Some three years earlier I had written:

> If this was mud and straw under a hot sun I would make bricks. Cool clay, I wedge you into smooth edged blocks. Neat. And progressively bigger. I hollow you out until I can sit in your pulled out edges. I sit inside the cave of clay.

That I guess is why I like keeping bits of scribble in files or folders. Diaries and journals are accessible and easier to look up, if dated on the outside cover or spine. I had no memory of writing about *a cave of clay,* but the embryonic writing was quite clearly there.

Through more exploratory writing, I discovered that pictures of sun-baked bricks emerged from deep in my childhood. Bricks of straw and clay baked in the scorching sun on the banks of the River Nile, some three thousand years ago.

A big impression has been left from my grandfather, intoning the Passover Service in Hebrew each year, followed by lengthy explanations in English. As children we followed the story in a picture book showing the Hebrew slaves making bricks for the Pharaoh's pyramid. The hard-hearted Pharaoh also makes an appearance in *Rope Mates*, so there was a link somewhere or other in my mind between the child, the pyramid building and the mud igloo. I always felt safe with that set of grandparents who looked after me a lot when I was a child. And the Passover Service is the one legacy from my Jewish upbringing that has survived into adulthood. It all makes sense now: how this strand of creativity and my buried memories had intertwined into a story which both delighted, surprised and comforted me.

MOROCCAN BRICKS

During one of my travels in Morocco, I was taking an early morning walk on the edge of the desert when I saw a pile of stacked mud bricks: bigger, squarer and chunkier than their English counterparts. Excitement rose from my belly to my hands which reached inside my rucksack and pulled out my notebook:

> There are two shallow pits. In the first is the mud, dark and moist. In the other is sand, dry grains which run through my fingers. A workman is mixing and rolling a mixture of mud and sand on the ground until it is a ball of muddiness. He then passes it from hand to hand until it is just like dough. Then it is back on the ground to knead and pull about into the shape he wants. He takes up handfuls and slaps it into formers: wooden frames subdivided into two. He fills this to the top, then mixes the next lot. By then the first is firm enough to tip out. He lines up his bricks in a semi-circle. They will lie in the sun for three days. By that time they will be dry and ready to use.
>
> (My Notes, 2011)

Rammed earth is the traditional building material in Morocco. No firing. Just the scorching heat of the sun. No transporting. They will be used to add a room to the camel owner's house just a hundred yards away.

METAPHOR AND ANGER

Wall Fictions gave me a scenario to deal with a difficult relationship when I could not resolve a conflict through conversation. I used an extended metaphor* simply through making more of a narrative with vivid imagery for an impotent fury. This was particularly affective: releasing me from obsessive angry feelings. On re-reading, the whole episode always comes flooding back from the past.

Could I have vented my anger more directly? Possibly. The other person did not live nearby, so it was not possible to meet up and have a confrontation. Phone calls got nowhere. She refused to listen or understand what I was saying, despite numerous attempts to talk to her. I tried to be reasonable, and with hindsight I think there was no right way to go about this. I wrote my pages and pages, and processed my feelings.

The only strategy that worked was the metaphorical piece and writing which follows. I named 'the other' Hilda which turned this person into a fictional character. This helped me gain some distance from my feelings and enabled the writing to flow. Fictionalizing our personal stories, of course, protects others and hides true identities, so that even the known person themselves might not recognize themselves.

Here is my fiction which helped me look at the situation from a different viewpoint:

Wall Fictions

You are a wall of crumbling bricks; each one compacted rubble, one on top of the other. The sheer force of all that compressed rubble keeps this towering structure in place. My wall to meet you is a steel wall. You can kick it as much as you like, dent it, bash it, if you get too close all you will see is yourself. Yes, someone riding full pelt on a steamroller.

After several months of no communication after the incident, when I felt misunderstood and misrepresented, this writing helped me deal with my relationship with Hilda. Drawing on this metaphor of two walls represented our conflicting roles: mine was the steel wall, her wall the crumbling bricks.

As I wrote the quality of the crumbling and compact heap of brick rubble became clearer, in contrast to my cold reflective steel wall. And then the whole scenario came visibly and vividly into my mind. And that space between the two walls was where the angry clash took place in our relationship.

This is how I had started before the images appeared. When I want to think of an image for another person, I quieten myself, go silent in my mind for a few moments, and then invite an image to present itself. That is how I came up with the wall for Hilda. I then built it as accurately as possible in my mind's eye: in size, shape and texture. I did the same for my own wall and that is how the steel wall popped into my head. Then I started writing about these two different walls.

The steel wall was my way of cutting off from Hilda. Using the image of a wall to represent each of us made it clear to me that her own structure was in place through the pressure of compacted rubble. This freed up some space in my mind to begin to wonder if within this compressed rubble there might be a vulnerability trapped inside, that the wall of crumbling bricks was a defence against a hidden hurt. All I had been aware of was her suppressed anger with me, shown through the *riding full pelt on a steamroller.* That was apt as I felt I had been *steamrollered* into her version of events. And my own anger was evident to me.

Observing Hilda in a different way as I wrote and explored my feelings shifted my anger because I started to feel some compassion. Whether my own take on her emotions was right or not, this empathetic view eased my discomfort and stopped me needing to talk about the situation, or have it go round inside my head in circles.

The writing, which had put up an imaginary wall for me, managed and then dissolved the anger. The narrative became sealed up in paragraphs and I called the whole lot *wall fictions.** I had owned my own anger, and I let go of any expectation of resolving that issue with Hilda. In time I removed my steel wall, and after a cooling off period, Hilda and I resumed contact.

BUILDING THE WALLS IN MY MIND

How did this wall writing come about?

With writing friends meeting in my house. After a discussion around the table, we developed the habit of drawing up a list of topics for writing. Sometimes we chose the same subject. Sometimes not. We then set a time limit and went off elsewhere to do a freewrite. Either indoors or in the garden.

Back at the kitchen table, we read our pieces to each other immediately with no censoring, and talked through our responses. Even when we used the same prompts to kickstart the writing, the results were varied in style and content.

That particular day, our discussion and subsequent writing had started because I said I felt a barrier had gone up between me, and the others.

I drew how I perceived this. My conversation I felt was directed around a straight line, which I perceived between them and me.

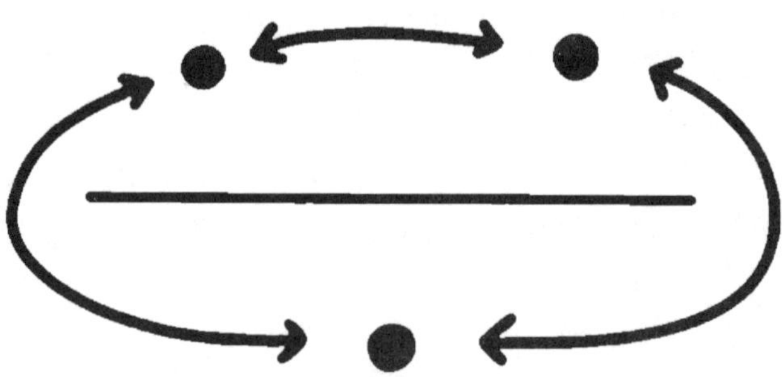

The sketch immediately translated itself into an obvious image of a wall. This energized all of us to go off and scribble away furiously. Here is how I ended my piece, which I read to the others:

The wall allows the meeting between you and the others.
At the wall there is an edge, here you may conduct your meetings.
(My Notes, 2006)

Although I was meaning 'me', I had used the second person pronoun, addressing myself with a 'you'. This also had the effect of distancing me, creating another objective 'me' as the 'you'. This was appropriate as I felt a new distance developing between me and the others.

My first imaginary wall was a thick one, about four feet high, so I could hop up and sit on the top with my feet swaying. In Virginia Woolf's novel *The Waves,* Bernard pointed out that two of his friends experienced 'the presence of other people as a separating wall' (Woolf 1966, p.57). I found, much to my surprise, that this way of using the wall had not essentially separated me from my friends. Mine was not a *separating* wall, but a *meeting* wall. I was sitting on top waiting to see how I would meet my friends, or how my friends would meet me. Wondering how would we continue meeting each other from our individual lives? Might we have to cross the in-between space? And if so how would we cross that in-between space to continue meeting each other from our individual lives? We were all intrigued with how the images had evolved in our writing and carried on exploring.

THE MUD WALL

I went on to imagine a wall for many of my friends, in exactly the same way. Here is how one friend shared the wall with me:

This wall is of mud
A mud wall with two bucket seats carved out
One on each side   We can sit horizontal to each other
but from different sides and talk

When I read those few lines to my regular writing friend Liz, there was a sigh of recognition from both of us. The mud rose smoothly and continuously out of the earth indicating a grounded and good friendship. She is younger than me and this was shown perfectly with the scooped out seats facing different ways and looking outwards; exactly right as she was establishing herself in adult years, and I was entering a much later stage with a grown-up daughter.

Yet we have a lot in common, so sharing the overall shape with the seats connected to the earth below was just right. Yet in the image there was no doubt we were separate. No muddling our boundaries. The sides and shape of these bucket seats made an enduring image for this particular friendship.

Indeed several years later, we looked at this piece of writing on my screen again. I have one of those chairs at my desk which swivels around. She said: *Look*, as she pivoted around to show me the configuration of these seats, *this is how I imagine the bucket seats, and it's not at all difficult to twist around slightly and talk.* This precisely fitted with how I had imagined we would see each other comfortably and talk easily.

WALL AND THE LOTUS BUSH

There was a day when Liz had a dream which she could not wait to tell me. Here it is in her own words:

> You gave me a light pink huge lotus flower in a glass box, and asked me to take it to a specific place which was far away from where you lived. You gave me directions though I'd never heard of it before, and told me I'd know when I found it. *Leave the box with the flower at this spot,* you said. I set off and walked for ages and was thinking I'd missed the place you wanted me to find. Then I arrived at the top of a hill and saw a flint

> wall completely covered in plants; against it a huge bush of the same flowers as the one you had given me to take there. I knew it was the place you wanted me to find. There, beneath the light pink flowering lotus bush was a carved dark wooden bench. On it a handwritten letter was lying. It was open. I put the glass box on the bench and in that instant knew I had to give you the message: this letter which I didn't read, and to tell you this dream.

Liz was the day-time messenger bringing me the dream with the unread letter for me. She had no doubt the message from my dream-self in her dream carried a spiritual dimension. Liz continued:

> When I got to the place I knew you wanted me to find, I was shocked and confused about why you would want me to bring this flower to this specific place, if you knew that the flowers were already growing there. And that's when I knew it was the right place. I knew that it wasn't about carrying the flower but about getting to the place. The journey was the point. You needed me to deliver this flower. I had to be the messenger. It was my job to place the flower where the letter was lying on the bench in front of the flint wall and bring the letter back to you; it was handwritten in black ink. I knew it was a love letter. I didn't read it because I would never understand it. The letter was for you to understand.
>
> (Liz's Notes, 2009)

Of course we both felt compelled to write from this dream. I needed to know what was written in this love letter; I had to write it myself. And not share it. That was private just like a real love letter. But here is how it ended:

Love tells the truth. Love finds the truth.
Love and truth. This is what we live for.

It reminded me of the last two lines of Keats' *Ode On A Grecian Urn*:

Beauty is truth, truth beauty, – that is all
Ye know on earth, and all ye need to know.

(Keats, 1819)

I was so surprised that writing this love letter left for me by that flint wall settled me, as if I had waited for it all my life. The perfectly petalled lotus flower is imbued with symbolism going far back into antiquity with stories from all over the world. Its beauty leads the eye inwards to a spiritual place. From my writing came a pure love; that is why writing this letter settled me. And with an ending that meant so much to me.

The act of writing and reading back to myself was nurturing, healing. I held in my hands a love letter perfectly expressed in a way only I might understand for myself.

WALLS AND RELATIONSHIP

Ending on this love letter written by myself to myself felt like coming full circle. Relating to myself before I relate to others. Knowing I need to be comfortable in my own being before I can relate well to anyone else. Perhaps I have to be my own best friend. Since describing how my own thinking changed through the writing of *Love & Loss,* I tap into a flowing kind of love I feel in the world as an energy which moves around and through me.

Knowing that I love myself as a complete and integrated emotional sentient being makes my own body my natural home. My body houses my flesh, blood and organs, the all of me including my belief system and approach to spirituality. I have an enclosed physical boundary, my skin: the wall of my skin.

Exploring my relationships with family and friends through conjuring up the wall as an extended metaphor has been so valuable. It has illuminated qualities with precision. The imaginative writing which created the mud igloo for my inner little girl gave me a safe and fictional home. When my outer life was overwhelmingly busy, I could retreat there in my mind and feel comforted.

This was healing for my child self who had not felt safe within the walls of the original family house. Undoubtedly the imprint of the early parental love I received permeated into my adult consciousness. And now as I approach the other end of my life, I find myself reflecting on the child I once was. But I also include my imaginative life through writing, which has been healing and integrative. And feels actually just as real.

Unlike Humpty Dumpty who had a great fall off a wall and could never be mended, this writing, however, does mend. Even the tricky relationships. Like the difficult encounter which presented me with a crumbling brick wall opposite my own steel one.

SHARING A BOUNDARY WALL

My house is semi-detached which means I share a party wall, in effect a sharing wall, with my neighbour. We often pass food to each other over the other boundary: the fence at the back of our long gardens. One day, as I was writing, there was a knock on the door:

Gifts

(for Hrvojka)

Arriving in my garden is my neighbour
with flour-dusted biscuits, moon-crescents
to melt in the mouth

She'd sewn and pinned a felt leaf
brooch onto her lapel   red
yellow-flecked   stitched

I've written about that leaf   I say
Here, have it   she fumbles, unclasps

this leaf   I am given   but
like the breeze I will flutter it into your hands
for you to place where it belongs

Monica Suswin

These biscuits are called *kiflice* by my Croatian neighbour, flavoured with vanilla she calls them, *vanil kifl.* Her baking is reminiscent of my maternal grandmother's pastries; over the garden fence Hrvojka spoke of the influence of mid-European cooking on her home country. And of course in turn my own Jewish grandmother (born 1890 in England) would have been influenced by her own mother who arrived in England as a girl from Poland.

The social giving and receiving of gifts and the business of thank-yous is the focus of the next chapter through a dramatic dialogue, *Tablecloth Talk*.

Writing To Do

Writing from my own impetuous and mischievous inner child provided me with a mud igloo – a landmark in my imaginative writing. A safe home in the theatre of my mind.

Theatre of the Mind

- Imagine a younger version of yourself (your very own inner child)
- Allow an image to come into your mind of a dwelling, a safe place
- Make it comfy and homely

- Let yourself see it in greater detail in your mind's eye
- Describe as you observe it through your imagination
- Write in simple language using a naïve style (see p.46)
- Write in the present tense
- Go with any changes which occur whilst writing

- When would be a good time to visit?
- Who would you like to be there with you?
- Would you like to be alone?
- What might you do when you are there?

- Write your story about this place

- See what links you can make with memories of your own childhood home
- Write about your need for this place for your adult self

Writing To Do

In the chapter, I wrote about Hilda, anger and an impasse. And how I wrote my way out of my feelings through the wall fictions. Below is an example of how a face-to-face conversation worked: feelings articulated from both sides, generous listening and discussion.

A good friend arrives for supper.
I can't chat while we eat – I am angry with you, I say.
She says: *I know you are. And I am angry with you.*

We ate our meal in silence, and then moved to the comfort of my den to start unpicking our angry feelings, talking for several hours. Certainly not a shouting kind of fury. More of a reaction from a misplaced and misfired response during a phone call. We unpacked all our thoughts about that conversation. Anger became replaced with understanding because we respected each other, and honoured the meeting between us.

Anger and Metaphor

The next time you feel angry with someone and there appears to be no sensible resolution, try some exploratory writing using a metaphor:

- Close your eyes, take a deep breath or two
- Invite an image to come into your mind for the other person
- Describe in detail the image
- Invite an image to come into your mind for yourself
- Describe in detail the image
- Create a dialogue between the images
- Use whichever pronouns feel apt (I, You, S/He, It/They)
- Imagine the space between these two images

Write a reflective piece about your feelings and go with any changes that occur during the process of writing. Include the quality of the space between you and the other person.

Anger and The Unsent Letter

Unbeknown to me, my friend who'd been angry with me had written me numerous Unsent Letters. *Why?* I asked. *Because I didn't want another phone call or Skype and we weren't going to see each other for a few weeks. Did you write my imaginary replies*, I asked. *No*, she said.

The imaginary reply is very much part of this process of correspondence.

- Write a letter (definitely not for sending) to someone where anger lingers (it may be from the past, the person may even be dead)
- Write an imaginary reply, as if from them to you
- Continue your correspondence until you reach some sort of peaceful conclusion

The Playfulness of Metaphor

Meta . . . phor (Greek: between and to carry)

Our language is made lively through metaphor, even when we do not realize. The vivid images conjured up with these verbs become metaphorical:

the discussion ping-ponged between them
she hammered her point home
he wilted under the onslaught

Metaphor Acted Out

Our imagination loves visual play and story-telling with character, voices, costumes and stage designs. And nowhere more so than in a Shakespearean play, particularly *A Midsummer Night's Dream*. Shakespeare invites the audience to enter yet one more dramatic pretence in the play within a play: here are actors as Athenian workmen in disguise. Snout, the tinker, presents himself as 'wall' and through 'the chink' in it, much whispering and absurdities are played out:

That I, one Snout by name, present a wall;
And such a wall, as I would have you think,
That had in it a crannied hole or chink,
Through which the lovers, Pyramus and Thisby,
Did whisper often very secretly.
This loam, this rough-cast and this stone doth show
That I am that same wall

(*A Midsummers Night's Dream*, v.i.)

Real Walls

Real walls are built of materials such as mud, stones or bricks and give shelter from heat or cold. Real walls provide dwellings for humans, for animals. Powerful political statements are symbolised in walls: of exclusion, of authority, of ownership and alienation of one type of peoples from another. Real walls control the free movement of people, keep people in, keep people out. My reflections on the political and historical perspectives of walls fed my understanding of their emotive resonances: as both the real thing and a metaphor.

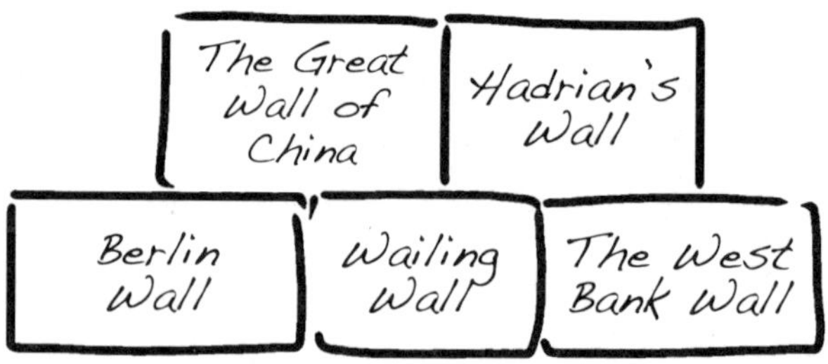

(see Notes p.109)

My Own African Wall

An African student was working in my garden. In Uganda, where he came from, he said he had built many brick walls. This was rather exciting and we planned a joint project: a wall to retain a bank. I learnt to mix sand, cement and water the African way. I was in seventh heaven helping to build the wall. I was less happy with the result of the pointing: my young man had smeared the mortar all over the brick edges. This was nothing like the neat grooves I have watched other builders do when applying wet mortar with a builder's trowel. *That's how we do it at home*, he told me cheerfully.

After he left, a builder suggested we top the African wall with some slabs to minimise the impact of the messy pointing and it would also provide seating. It looked really good.

The following winter was extremely cold and the slabs loosened. Another maintenance man re-fixed them, but the wall and the slabs were at odds with each other. He told me he had used a spirit level and repositioned them all because the wall wasn't straight.

I stopped being so pleased with the newly secured seating. The first builder who had relied on using his own eyes produced the visually effective work with the seating. It reminded me that the technically competent approach does not always work best.

I apply this approach to my writing: intuitive judgement and trust. Not technique.

CHAPTER 4

Tablecloth Talk

The writing in this chapter explores an uneasy feeling after a weekend gathering of friends to celebrate a significant birthday. I tackled this discomfort by making a fiction of the social event, creating a drama interspersed with prose, featuring characters in an imaginative setting. What underpins the writing, however, are real feelings: the kind of emotions which leak out in our interactions with each other. But at the time, as an event unfolds, these may not even be identified or acknowledged. My writing exposed a set of particular feelings and their cause. These are classic boundary issues which arise between friends of long standing and within families.

I started out with a creatively therapeutic approach to deal with a residue of discomfort after a weekend away, spent with friends I had known for many years. The narrative led the way and when finished, my writing restored my sense of equilibrium and comfort. Within the frame-work I set myself, I worked with freewrites, character studies, mind maps, dialogue, lists and unsent letters.

The issues in real life only surfaced after the event and an exchange of telephone conversations, letters, and e-mails. I had enjoyed the weekend so this aftermath took me aback, and then left me feeling uncomfortable.

When something jars with friends, I find it often takes a few days for my feelings to surface. At the time, I was just taking in what was being said. I would have preferred face-to-face contact but we all lived too far apart and I could not see any point in continuing any more real exchanges. This was a completely different situation to the one I found myself in with Hilda (see pp.53-55) but it still had me reaching for paper and pencil. Initially I resorted to my faithful strategy of unsent letters to deal with my disquiet.

A twist revealed itself in my own imaginary replies to the unsent letters which surprised me so much that I thought it would work well as fiction. Though like many disclaimers in novels, there is no resemblance in the story or the characters to any real event or person. This story became based on a completely different set of circumstances, and characters who bore no likeness to my friends, protecting their identities. What I transferred were the emotional undercurrents and that made this exploratory writing particularly worthwhile and authentic.

It is not a literary story*, although the process to set it up had everything in common with the early planning stages of writing fiction. All the decisions I took about writing styles, however, came intuitively from my inner wise writer. The insights came later.

A GIFT NOT WELL RECEIVED

In the first place, I wrote an unsent letter to one of the friends and my imaginary reply. This expressed what I really felt and settled on the feeling that our family gifts had not been well received. Even though I am experienced with this kind of writing, the correspondence which emerged surprised me.

AUTHOR AND NARRATOR

In literary fiction, the voice of the author* needs to be differentiated from the narrator's voice* as the story is told. To maintain the integrity of the writing, the author's task is usually to stand aside and let their narrator and characters do their job within the perspective they hold in the narration. It is easy to tell when authors go astray: if a character has access to information beyond their brief in the story, or the reader detects the author's own views, then the writer has not distanced themselves enough, and has crept into the text uninvited.

In personal creative therapeutic writing, however, I am definitely the writer as author and narrator of my own devised stories. I could easily have worked up a short story. That was not my purpose, but I was tempted. Then I would have needed to make more of a dramatic curve and find literary ways to indicate the nuances of the social relationships.

NARRATIVE: FIRST STAGE

On completing the unsent letters to my friend, I went on to invent a fictional scenario. Creating a mind map (as used in Chapter 2), I worked out theme, setting and characters. But I did not have a set idea of direction or form the writing would take.

Novelists often say their characters and plots evolve in ways they, as authors, do not necessarily control. I found, as a lively energy fed into my imagination, that the narrative looked after itself, and found its own shape. In fact I realised this weekend so fully that the scenes and characters became alive in my mind as I wrote pages sequencing activities. This part of the process was creative and enjoyable. I interwove those imagined events with similar memories of other such gatherings. Although much of that exploratory writing has not been included here, it contributed to help me imagine the fiction. My own need to write about a lukewarm *thank you* became satisfied.

Getting an interesting angle on social celebrations, one of my characters became an anthropologist. He would give the story an observational viewpoint as the story unfolded. He became the key to unlocking the content. I gave myself a back-story for characters, settings and an event in a similar way a novelist might also do. My anthropologist became Jake, a Master's student and I kind-of-turned into his mum, Gwyneth. Husband and dad Tom does not appear in the story.

As the title of the chapter suggests, there is the presence of the tablecloth; pristine white, laid crisply over a table for a celebration, representing best-behaviour expected.

Tablecloth Talk implies polite social conversation. My writing, through the intercessions of Jake's observations, succeeded in whipping that tablecloth off the table. On the surface I was playing, but the writing got underneath the social structure to reveal the interactions of a group of friends.

CONTEXT OF STORY

The dramatic event is the celebration of a fiftieth birthday: Patricia's, second wife to Francis. He is a long-term friend of Gwyneth and Tom and part of a network of friends dating back to university who meet up several times a year. Francis and Patricia invited their friends as weekend guests to Southwold on the Suffolk coast. Present too were their nine-year old twins.

CHARACTERS

I visualized the characters and gave each of them a personality, history and place in the narration. I chose names, ages and worked out relationships so I could imagine why they were present at the weekend. Once I had transposed my own social experience over to these people, they presented their own ways of handling the issues I was aiming to address. The main characters easily settled into the mother and son.

Gwyneth is in her fifties and I based her on a composite of women I knew. She was definitely not me as the writing progressed, and became her own character in the text. I allowed her to enjoy writing, which meant I was able to have her do all the writing explorations I would set for myself. She had had a relationship with Francis (their weekend host) at university and later married Tom.

Jake is twenty-six years old, the youngest of their three children (two older sisters do not feature in the story). As a student, he is living at home to help with his finances and he joined his parents for the weekend. He played a key role in the text; exposing the hidden feelings through dialogue and his carefully observed notes.

THE TWINS

At the start of my thinking, nine-year old twins (the children of Francis and Patricia) played a much bigger part. Their role, however, became less and less significant. If I had been writing a literary story I would have included details to show their sweet nature: Jake hoisting them onto his broad shoulders and the pair decorating little cup cakes for each of the guests.

It was quite a wrench cutting the twins out. Nevertheless it was good imagining them because in the end they were relevant in the unsent letter exchange between Gwyneth and Patricia. There was a counterpoint to their absence which mattered to this final denouement.

TABLECLOTH

The tablecloth was white damask and spread over the long oval dining room table by Patricia; beautifully laid with silver, wine glasses, napkins, candlesticks and a couple of small vases of hedgerow red berries and winter evergreen leaves. And fir cones sprayed gold for table decorations by the twins. Like the wall in the previous chapter, the tablecloth entered the drama with its own voice, proving chatty.

PLACE

Characters always need to be grounded in a real place. That may sound obvious. But I have read plenty of novels where characters appear to float around. As a reader, I need to feel anchored in a geographical, physical space. So that I can enter a three dimensional setting.

I needed two locations as I wanted Gwyneth and family to have a long car journey. I set Patricia and Francis in Suffolk near the sea, a coastline I knew. They lived in a large detached 1920s house with plenty of space for some guests. Gwyneth, Tom and Jake, however, stayed in a B & B. They had a long drive from one side of the country to the other: west to east, which placed their home in South Wales.

The action takes place after the weekend: Gwyneth at her functional kitchen table, square, scrubbed pine top. There she talks to Jake and writes on her lined pad of paper whilst Jake tapped away on his keyboard.

With places and characters more or less settled, I was ready to explore. All this setting up (and more) was necessary as the foundation for the narrative.

THE EXPLORATORY WRITING

How did Jake fit into my personal scenario? That was my first task. I started with a few questions:

Me: Are you perhaps the son I don't have?

Jake: My mum is Gwyneth and so I can't be your son. We get on really well that is why I can live at home with her and Dad. I love both my parents.

Me: Are you possibly my alter ego: the academic inner other me who never went down that path?

Jake: Could be. Not much to say about that since you are my creator.

Me: But not creator as in say: . . . your mother?

Jake: No I've told you I have a mother in the story. I am not really enjoying conversing with you. You are distracting and diverting me from my purpose. Please let me get on with my work. I have to type up my notes. Excuse me.

I did not get very far with that. Terse as only people in their twenties can be, when they do not want to tell you anything. Although I believe he is a delightful young man and quite talkative with his own mum. Clearly not representing a would-be son.

Since early field studies, social anthropology has had a big shift in emphasis from studying far away countries. Even back in the 1950s, our culture was seen to be just as open to study as any other (Maus 2002, p.83). So Jake is studying the tribe he belongs to: middle class contemporary Britain. And he intended to submit his dissertation on observations of celebratory events such as this weekend.

Jake made copious research notes about the celebration: details which interested him about the social interactions and what he perceived as rituals. He was particularly interested in the reciprocity of gift giving (including the contributions and giving of food), and how hospitality was given by their hosts.

I have never studied anthropology and have no idea how a real student might make such notes so I have speculated on what this list might be like and include a few that my reading made me aware were significant areas of study:

Jake's Field Study Notes

Gift: Ceramic vase from local pottery – taken with us to give

Gifts: Ours – Contributions: wine, smoked salmon, cheeses

Gifts: All Guests – Contributions: food, wine, personal present

Hosts: Provide Saturday evening celebratory meal

Hosts: Provide setting for all meals and socialising

Hosts: Provide some accommodation. We stay in B & B.

Ritual: 'Happy Birthday' sung, candles lit on decorated cake

Ritual: Kisses and hugs – beginning and end of weekend

Table: Formally laid with white tablecloth in dining room

Bonds: Reinforced with weekend activities
strengthened by future plans for next ritual gathering

WEEKEND DISCUSSED

After arriving home, Jake and Gwyneth chatted over a cup of coffee about the weekend. I am going to give them what I can only say is an example of some really terrible dialogue. A real fictional writer would not get away with some of this.

One of the basic rules I learnt from an actor many years ago was never, never commit the faux pas of writing the equivalent of: *the gun I am holding in my right hand is loaded and pointed at you.** In creative writing, that is unforgivable: a No-No. The audience, or reader, needs to receive information subtly not with a clunk of the obvious. Writing needs to show the action and not tell it through obvious description. That is the rule of 'show not tell' taught on all creative writing courses.

For personal writing, however, I have no need to be subtle. The following was intentional and permissible. I am not even attempting spare or understated dialogue. Quite the opposite. What I wanted to do was serve my fictional purpose of exposing the hidden feelings. Here I do just that:

Jake's Niggle

Jake: I didn't get the feeling that Patricia liked her present.

Gwyneth: Hard to say, her *thank you* was a bit quick. Lukewarm, even. And she never mentioned it again. I thought we'd given her a lovely gift.

Jake: Well there were a lot of presents piled up on the sideboard, I guess. What about all that smoked salmon, cream cheese and ham, not to mention the bottles of wine. Did you get a *thank you* for that?

Gwyneth: We all mucked in Jake. Didn't really expect anything over the top from Patricia. Francis was clearly delighted with everyone's goodies. I thought we had a great weekend away. Thought you really enjoyed yourself.

Jake: I did. Enjoyed it lots. Great to see everyone. Just left with a niggle. That's all.

GIFTS AND THANKS

Jake had drawn his Mum's attention to one of his observations. The giving and receiving of gifts is common in most societies. In our British way of life, the 'thank you' for gifts and for hospitality is part of social interactions. A study of 'expressions of gratitude' highlighted 'acquired different habits' for 'politeness' in different cultures.* As customs vary from country to country, I qualify my take on this because the UK is where I live, and my experience of other cultures is limited to holidays.

Whilst Jake was typing up his notes on the computer, Gwyneth poured herself another coffee and settled down to write the thank you card to Patricia and Francis. She expressed her genuine pleasure about the weekend with ease. Left the card on the table for Tom and Jake to sign and write a line or two; addressed and stamped the envelope.

I know that however much I might persuade myself that I do not in fact need a 'thank you', when it is missing I certainly notice. Something feels unfinished, unappreciated, taken for granted: that the present did not please.

Getting Jake to address this issue with his mum, helped me address my own misgivings about gifts given or sent and never acknowledged. I discussed this with other friends of my age and found this was a common experience. I was, indeed, exploring an issue with weight.

Here are Jake's notes looking back over the weekend, helping me get essential information across:

Jake's Observation: i

Ritual: effusive and loud exchanges when guests hand over food contributions and wine to Francis, the host. This caused a lot of laughter. Francis received wine graciously.

Patricia was not gracious about receiving her gifts. Waved a hand towards the dining room, presents put on the sideboard.

Presents opened when we ate birthday cake on Saturday evening. Her 'thanks yous' were under-whelming. Noted.

Patricia is younger than Francis. Second wife. I remember their wedding when I was sixteen.

Mum is now dutifully writing her thank you card. She'll probably leave a space at the bottom for Dad and me to write a line. Family ritual. Noted.

Two devices in this chapter help the observational angles addressed:

* fictionalising a personal story
* inventing a character as an anthropologist

These strategies allowed me as writer to distance myself from my own emotionally charged subject matter, and helped me to express my own niggles in a more creative way.

The dialogue which follows is between Jake and the inanimate object of the tablecloth. This started off as pure fun: on the surface I was playing, but by the end the writing became serious. My real issues underlying social gatherings were exposed.

FLASHBACK: JAKE TALKS TO THE TABLECLOTH

TC: I hope the guests noticed me underneath all those fancy platters of food and the silver cutlery and candlesticks. Patricia was pleased with me I'm sure. I lay flat under all that weight. And when I lie quiet, crisp and white, I listen to the voices.

Jake: I certainly noticed you. And I listened to what was said, and even more to what was not said. I'm writing up a lot of notes.

TC: I took it all in like blotting paper. No-one would dare write with pen and ink on me. Though it didn't take long before someone spilt a glass of red wine over me. Patricia jumped up and dealt with it. She was very polite – that hid how much I was insulted. 'Not to worry, not to worry', she kept repeating. That's not what I would have said, but there's nothing I could say at table. Good to get a chance to tell you now how fed up I was.

This parallel of wine with ink came in the writing not through any thinking before I wrote. That is how the writing often works when it flows with juxtapositions of images coming naturally and fitting the occasion.

Jake: Well that's how we are at table. Polite. Best behaviour. At least that's how we start out. That's exactly what I'm observing and describing. My dissertation is about how people meet around the table and the rituals that have evolved in different societies. That's what makes up the social fabric of a culture. And in our family life, we learn social behaviour and the rules. I like to notice the looks too.

These were the second set of notes Jake made:

Jake's Observation: ii

I noticed Patricia give Mum a sideways look

I noticed Francis look at Mum

I noticed Dad did not notice either look

I avoided looking at Mum for about ten minutes after this

I don't know what these looks meant

I missed any look Mum might have given. Unfortunate.

CONVERSATION CONTINUES:

Jake: Yes, politeness covers up too for what is not said. We humans cover all sorts of things up. Eye contact says a lot, if you can read it. I'm all in favour of whipping you off and looking underneath for knee nudging or little kicks given under the table.

TC: The table is under me stupid boy, scratched and gouged from being old. Francis calls it *patina* when Patricia complains. *It's how tables are meant to be,* he says. And from what I can understand it's where you share your common humanity because whether a human is old or young, rich or poor, everyone gets hungry and people have been sitting at tables like me of one sort or another for a long time.

Jake: Francis is absolutely right.

TC: You know I only serve the family for special occasions.

Jake: I thought as much.

TC: After that politeness, everyone gets louder and interrupts each other, then there's that noise you call laughter. Then no-one really cares about my perfect whiteness and in no time at all I am grubby. Some humans wipe their sticky fingers on my folds when their napkin has fallen unnoticed onto the floor and they don't want to show themselves up by stooping down to pick it up.

Jake: You're just like us humans you know. We don't stay clean for long.

TC: I notice you humans start out the day clean and tidy in the morning and end the day used up, sweating, smelly. Mine go upstairs to hide away in their containers.

Jake: We all need containers where we can rest. I expect your humans shower if they are that smelly. Anyway you have a drawer I suppose where you are kept and we have beds.

TC: When I'm out of the drawer I have a purpose. It's to cover what's underneath. Cover the imperfections of the oak table.

Jake: You also look very special and smart. Like we do in our best clothes. We like to cover up those abrasive, imperfect moments we have, which show how difficult and complicated we find each other. Mum's very good at saying the right thing to smooth over those awkward times.

TC: Smoothing over the surface. Isn't that what I'm about? As soon as I'm laid on the table all creases go, as soon as everyone sits around me and lay their napkins on their laps everyone appears happy. I make people happy. At the end of the meal when I am dirtied and crumpled and unhappy myself, I will be put in the washing machine. And when I am clean and ironed, I will be put away in the drawer until the next time. I am there to remind all who sit around me that harmony around the table is what these occasions are about. Happy times. They might not last long but as long as I am perfectly placed all will be well. And all may be well again the next time.

Jake: You are a wise old thing. When I have my own home I'll make sure Mum gives me one of you. You do a lot of good in the home.

This writing, I found, also cleansed my mind through exposing the issues to the light of day. Jake has now fulfilled his function in the story.

The last stage of the writing addressed the nub of the matter:

GWYNETH'S UNSENT LETTERS AND REPLIES

Without Jake's earlier comments, Gwyneth would not have given much more thought to Patricia. Once alerted to this lack of a good *thank you* for their gift on the part of their hostess, she could no longer ignore the quiet rumble from the back of her mind.

Gwyneth had written her thank you card easily and quickly, but as she sat there finishing her coffee, she found herself ruminating on how Jake had voiced a discomfort she had been vaguely aware of, and dismissed as trivial. But now she felt she was crossing that invisible boundary of comfort towards discomfort. (And I as the writer-proper was reminded of shifting boundaries).

Gwyneth reached for her pad and pen:

Dear Patricia,

You didn't thank us for our contributions. Your *thank yous* for all the presents appeared perfunctory. Despite all your lovely hospitality, you showed little magnanimity of spirit.

We came laden with food offerings and several bottles of wine. We drove from one side of the country to the other. We paid our way as guests do, as well as joining in with the washing up, the hoovering and tidying. We gave you all our own normal *thank yous*. You appear to want all the *thank yous*. Don't you? How come you are so greedy for them?

Puzzled,
Gwyneth

As I revised this first letter of Gwyneth's, I noticed every single sentence had initially been expressed as a question. Questions that in this imaginary format Patricia was not going to address.

In the first draft of Gwyneth's letter, the questions had been:

How come you appear to want all the *thank yous*?
How come you didn't thank us for our contributions?

Did we have to pay our way, as well as join in
with the washing up, the hoovering and tidying?

I changed those questions into the statements which appear in the unsent letter as it appears here. Far more powerful. It meant Gwyneth addressed Patricia directly and enabled my fictitious character, and me, to own indignant feelings.

After that, I wrote as if Patricia was replying:

Dear Gwyneth,

What's your problem? I did thank you for the beautiful vase you gave me. I thanked you for the food, which you added to the pile like everyone else. I heard Francis thank Tom for the wine. I work hard at home and at work. No-one works as hard as I do. It was a lot of work getting ready for the weekend. We are glad you, Tom and Jake came.

Patricia

And I carried on with this letter writing from both their points of view:

Dear Patricia,

I'm glad about that. I do have a problem. Maybe I missed some of those *thank yous*. You're not the only one who works hard. We all work hard in our own ways. Your *thank yous* were short and quick. I've no real idea whether you liked any of your presents – ours or others.

Gwyneth

Dear Gwyneth,

Of course I liked the vase. A perfectly lovely present. I did not need to thank you more. You needed to thank me. We gave the party. I do not need to thank you.

Patricia

Everyone thanked you lots, Patricia. You astonish me.

Gwyneth

And here the tone and sentiment make a change: a pointed one.

Dear Gwyneth,

I am the taker, and receiver. I provide the warmth of the home, the polished silver, the flower arrangements, the ironed tablecloth and napkins, all that goes on the table. My hard work means I do not have to thank anyone. I expected you to come laden with contributions and a present for me. After all it was my fiftieth. So why should I thank you for what I expect?

Patricia

ps: Francis was in charge of all the arrangements not me.

And now comes the nub of the matter; the underlying feelings:

Dear Patricia,

Yes, we were in e-mail contact with Francis about all the planning. You don't do e-mail. Is that what this is about? That Francis and I have a special friendship.

Gwyneth

Dear Gwyneth,

I know Francis is fond of you. Gives you time whenever the lot of us meet up. When I'm usually spending my time with the twins or in the kitchen.

Patricia

Dear Patricia,

Francis is attentive to you. Look at the lovely party he arranged.

All for you.

Gwyneth

Dear Gwyneth,

Francis is also attentive to you. When I am looking after the twins he still finds time for you.

Patricia

Dear Patricia,

I can't believe this is what it's about. You're not jealous of me surely? Anyway the best thing about the weekend was getting to know the twins a lot better. They are great girls.

Gwyneth

Dear Gwyneth,

You share something with Francis I don't.

Patricia

Dear Patricia,

Of course I do; we go a long way back. That's what friendships are about. Sharing something you might not share with your partner or other friends. That's what makes them special.

Tom has no difficulty that Francis and I are fond of each other. I have no designs on Francis. Truly I haven't. We've always been friends. Really Patricia I can't believe this is what it's about. I enjoy my friendship with you and with Francis. There is and never has been any threat.

So are you just plain jealous? Is that what's going on? Well I never, this never even occurred to me. Still it wouldn't hurt you to show some *thank yous* if the two are related. It beggars belief.

Gwyneth

Dear Gwyneth,

Well we've had this out so the air is cleared. I still don't have to thank you. And that's the point.

Patricia

Writing this convoluted and concocted series of letters was good. Even though fictional, everything felt fully imagined and real: the social circle of friends, the anthropology student son, and the personalities of Patricia and Gwyneth.

Even with my completely different circumstances but alongside these imaginary characters, I too felt the air had been cleared. I was amazed at the jealousy slipping in sideways. This had never occurred to me in my own friendship with another couple. The letters touched the relevant points and were playful to write.

Through this exploration, I learnt that what really mattered were the feelings underpinning the story. And through the character of Patricia, I understood more about my relationship with a female friend.

The attraction was not necessarily about sex, but about time given to Gwyneth (aka me) and perceived as time taken away from herself. From that revelation, it then became apparent there was a link between Patricia's jealousy and a lack of graciousness as the hostess receiving a present.

Investigating what started out as a niggle mattered to me, enough to find a way to write about it. What is significant to me may not bother another person, but we all have small upsets, or even ones we deem petty. But if they will not go away and cannot be stopped, then respect for writing about them may bring more understanding and a deeper revelation. And allow for a letting go of irritated feelings.

My inner wise writer came into her own through an intuitive grasp of the writing process. But it was not until later that I understood the effectiveness of all these pieces.

The lack of expressed delight in receiving took away from the pleasure of giving. The resolution of feelings gave the writing a full and rounded shape. This was a creative and satisfying exercise giving me more understanding of the people involved in my own circle of friends and dealing with the issue of gift giving.

Coming to terms with my feelings meant I had to write a lot of detailed description in order to frame the dramatic content of my fiction, much of which I have not included. The transfer of the main issue to those two families then lived vicariously in my mind. And I resolved my feelings about the real discomfort I had experienced in the creative and therapeutic writing. The total experience of the writing was vital to this process.

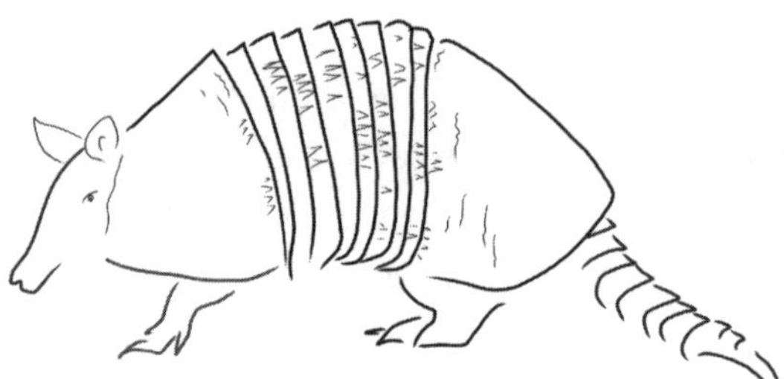

Writing To Do

- Choose an awkward memory of an event: one which has unsettled or disturbed you
- Name the underlying feelings as precisely as possible
- Describe the setting, the time period
- Draw an arc on a plain piece of paper
- Plot the action, however minimal from beginning to end

Now write the story:

- Experiment with tense: present or past
- Decide who is telling the story
- Write in first, second or third person
- Read over and redraft
- Put it away for a while
- Rewrite until you are happy with the result

Fictionalizing Memories

One Approach to Start Your Story

The Setting

Close your eyes, take yourself back to the scene you may have written about from the exercise (previous page), or another event. Ground your description in the place with whatever details feel relevant.

The Characters

Who exists in that memory? Give everyone and yourself fictional names. This really helps the characters to develop. Describe them: experiment with the first, second or third person. My character Gwyneth, originally based on myself, finally turned into a composite of various women I knew.

Narrative

Write one incident or several. Write as separate parts of the story. Then think about links, or ways to get from one scene to another. Write as it comes. Write in the past. Write in the present. Write from the point of view of different characters. Write as the character who mostly represents yourself. Choose what works effectively. Experiment with style, language and voice.

Backstory

Knowing the background of your characters, the event, and what has happened before is useful to ground your narrative, even if you don't use the information. At first write randomly about all of this. It may feed into the story you tell. Writing character descriptions will make you more familiar with their stories, and with what may have happened before the chosen narrative you plan to tell. I spent time on what my twins did in the story: helping with flower arrangements for the table and how Jake swung them onto his shoulders. None of that appeared in the drama but it added to the weight of the visual description of the setting. And the twins were mentioned in a pointed comment in a letter from Patricia.

The Story

At this stage don't worry about grammar, punctuation and correct use of language. Redraft later with extra writing: more description, maybe some dialogue. Check your use of senses. Redraft with an eye to re-ordering your material and marking where the story starts and ends. It may not be at the obvious beginning. Make another more detailed arc for the dramatic action. When you feel your story is all told, edit for the finished style.

Another approach is just write one sentence and let the rest flow

Writing TO DO and NOT TO DO

- If your writing bores you – *STOP*
- If you feel an *ought* about writing – *STOP*
- If your writing is *stirring your emotions* more than you want – *STOP*

BUT

- If you feel blocked – pause, breathe deeper
- Write about THE MOMENT NOW to stimulate the flow to start again

AND

- If more feelings surface, weave them into the story if appropriate
- Write everything down, even if it doesn't feel relevant at the time

Putting writing to one side for a time can be really helpful. Your unconscious mind will do the work for you as you go about other things. *Sleeping on it* also has merit and can clarify your intentions. Write your diary in the morning and you may return to your writing with new energy, or you may just drop that piece entirely.

- Trust your writing and follow where it wants to go
- Use the range of creative and therapeutic strategies in this book
- Set yourself projects that really interest you
- Scribble away with no concern for an end result

Dramatic dialogue, letter writing, using metaphors have contributed to character and scene development for my own exploratory process and been surprisingly illuminating.

- Learn to judge the kind of writing which helps you express your authentic self
- Where? Who? What? How? Why? Five questions to ask about any story.

On the whole this way of writing is fun and insightful. There are times, however, when you may feel vulnerable. Give yourself permission to write from that vulnerable place, but look after yourself and consider seeking support from a trusted friend or professional practitioner.

Above all take responsibility for what is good for you to write about
And what you choose to share

Haiku for Sally

Haiku: a short thematic Japanese form traditionally about nature
Using a stylized 5-7-5 format of syllables.
The third line providing a satisfying twist in meaning

In the West, we might follow these traditional rules but deviate on subject matter. My haiku for Sally sticks to the 5-7-5 format of syllables, but do not necessarily follow the traditional rules of writing about a season as this first one shows. It came from a newspaper cutting Sally had sent me in the post:

buy one fish 'n' chips
for price of two   get second
absolutely free

As I lived a two hour drive from the hospice, I only visited once a fortnight. I wondered what Sally was seeing from the window of her room and began to text daily about what I was seeing from my own bedroom window in the morning. The garden was beginning to burst into blossom and flowers; we had had a long winter and spring was late in 2013. It felt natural to turn my *Good Morning* texts into haiku.

Fresh and something new every day, Sally said, *a simple form.*

a haiku a day
to amuse for a moment
sent to you   by text

Here is one she enjoyed:

silver seed balls   lift
off ten thousand yellow heads
sun kissed   dandelions

I did not know then that it was dandelions she had made to scan during a poetry game rewriting Wordsworthian verses, which the family had played in the Lake District during their last holiday in April. Sally had come up with:

When all at once I saw a crowd
a host of golden dandelions.

Here are a couple more of my haiku:

through the window pane
white blossom   sun softens skin
sap rises   purple plums

*   *   *

sharp nosed foxy sniffs
these words today   pads down path
burnished tail   no hot stink

CHAPTER 5

Writing: a Shifter of Boundaries

Writing a haiku is a disciplined and focussed way of using boundaries for a precise number of syllables and words on separate lines: a homing in on one tiny aspect of life. Other writing by hand, however, may sprawl across pages and pages of diaries and journals with no concern for boundaries. Redrafting can allow even more unpacking and exploration of subject matter. If boundaries are about the discipline of concise thought, contained emotional expression and a distinct style, then with *creative and therapeutic writing* that comes with the process of editing when transforming the writing into a particular form or style.

Writing releases the power of the memory kept locked up inside the skull. It releases feelings long forgotten and deepens those memories. Loosens the emotional boundaries. And most importantly, it is able to transform discomfort into comprehension of tricky situations, and at times compassion for *the other*. Writing, I find, is a great shifter of my own inner boundaries and increases my awareness of who I am.

During a stressful period in my fifties I had a real need to cross the border into my imaginative life: the story of *the mud igloo* provided me with a much needed place of safety inside my mind. With my writing I met a small girl inside me who needed fun and comfort, and with exploratory writing my adult self derived significant insights. I do not assume that writing has the absolute power to heal the imprint of inadequate parenting from early life. But I do believe that fictions like this form new creative memories in the mind. My *mud igloo* is a parallel reality to the brick-built house I live in. And I can visit this imaginary place any time I wish. It stays intact in my mind because I have inhabited it imaginatively through my writing.

The long sea house from my dream writing similarly stays in my imagination and represented a different life to the one my parents might have chosen for me. Creating a purely physical boundary from parents starts from the moment of birth when the umbilical cord is cut from the mother. It is a long and very slow separation through childhood to adulthood. Healthy emotional separation may happen with maturity. Or some, like myself, may take a lifetime to achieve this. My dream writing which started this book, and later writing illuminated how my boundaries had established a far more flexible outlook as I grew into adulthood.

Fictionalizing memories of real events I found respected the personal story, yet stayed true and authentic to the underlying feelings. Stories which are simple to start with those enduring words *once upon a time* can be fun as well as give clarity. Once characters, place and situation are in place, writing may flow easily. And satisfaction may also be achieved through gaining an alternative approach to a problematic scenario. Making a fiction of an autobiographical narrative allows for a distancing approach, yet creates a bridge to the real feelings underpinning the narrative.

Writing the Hilda story in *Wall Fictions* helped capture bottled-up anger with a vivid metaphor which revealed vulnerability. It is impossible to really get inside the boundary of another's skin, yet this writing allowed me to do so imaginatively. And then the impasse I felt in real life dissolved into compassion. The other metaphor of the armadillo with its leathery shield-shaped scales also hid a soft vulnerable inner life. Watching how these metaphors turned over preconceptions about other people has been a real eye-opener. And in both cases, I observed how my emotional boundaries shifted through *creative and therapeutic writing.*

Generosity is involved in the giving and receiving of gifts. Dramatic scenes, dialogue and letter writing in *Tablecloth Talk* gave me further understanding about a baffling social situation focussing on *thank yous*. Surprising feelings were named and revealed, then resolved to the satisfaction of the characters in the story. And I found this resolution transferred to myself as the issue cleared in my thoughts. Although at the beginning of any writing adventure, I have no idea what the outcome might be.

All my explorations allowed feelings to shift their edges within my own emotional life. In the second chapter I certainly valued defining my own personal boundaries through my exploratory writing, then acknowledging their existence and realizing they are more complex than I first thought.

The writing in *Shifting Boundaries* has given me a voice for owning my separate and individual self whilst staying in relationship with others. Appreciation for close friendships and becoming ever more aware of the emotional space between the 'I' of me and the 'you of another' has led to more recognition and understanding of my connections. And appreciating that my feelings are often on the move depending on circumstances.

With friends, I am often in the position of suggesting different ways of writing. I am careful not to invade someone else's boundary as well as being mindful of not intruding with my own opinions when we are discussing issues which crop up in conversation. But when we go round in circles or get nowhere in our deliberations, I cannot help but say that writing might be a good idea. A really good idea.

Writing helps me to make sense when I have grappled with areas of my life which appeared to be overwhelming, chaotic, and unmanageable. I really value the boundary of words to stop the shifting around of thoughts, and then in that process stemming confusion or clarifying a puzzling situation. And finding a shift in my feelings and thoughts which change my perspective and may solve the issue.

This process of writing is amazing when given due respect. I sit quietly, alone and with my diary; I breathe, I follow the stream of words at their own speed, sometimes quick, sometimes slow, and find it is the writing itself which gives me answers that change how I think and respond to the conundrums in everyday life and relating to others when it is not straightforward.

Looking for boundaries with observational descriptions was somewhat more straightforward and has made me look at architecture more keenly and watch how the light played with the sea and land on my travels to the Arctic. Writing about infinity, space and time taught me to think clearly and was valuable in stretching the boundaries of my intellect to appreciate what I could understand.

Shifting Boundaries is concluding, so now I come up against its own boundary of summing up what I have gained from my exploratory writing. It has given me quite a broad definition on its own terms of its flexible nature, how our emotions may transform through writing, how writing is shaped with spaces, and how life leads to, and then over the inevitable threshold of death. And I will not be able to write about what that is like. But I have been able to write about the death of others which helps to acknowledge what someone's life has meant to me. And in that process face my own inevitable death.

The boundary of this final chapter will end on this page with this full stop and some words in a bracket.

(the end)

But this wasn't the end to my thinking about boundaries ...

Epilogue
Covid 19 and Boundaries

As I finish this book on boundaries and how they shift around, a dreadful disease has spread throughout the world breaching the immune systems of human beings and with no regard for the borders of countries. Every life has been impacted. Covid 19 has redrawn the boundaries for all of us in our personal and working lives.

Coronavirus invades the human body and replicates its molecular structure to cause havoc with our vital physiological need to breathe. In order to control the spread of disease and limit deaths, we have been instructed into lockdown. This global pandemic may even give us a portal to a different way of organizing ourselves and society. But only with hindsight will we know if this is a pivotal moment in our history.

This epilogue is a resumé of my writing about boundaries and Covid 19 for the three months of March, April and May 2020:

MARCH

My lockdown, the restriction of my personal boundaries to remain within the four walls of my house and in my garden started after two events: a birthday party and a funeral. The birthday celebrated my grandson crossing an early milestone in the life of a child: turning from two to three years old. No longer a toddler, definitely now a little boy wearing a red and white checked shirt and blue jeans. Whilst the funeral was for a friend dying from cancer at fifty-nine, reluctantly reaching the end of her life.

Those of us who had been part of a supportive group felt she had prepared us for the news of deaths every day.

Emotions are spilling over psychological boundaries into panic and anxiety. I cannot book a Waitrose online shop for weeks. People are hoarding food. *Shelves are empty*, I am told. I am meant to be a vulnerable over seventy-year old, but that is not my reality.

During this self-isolation, we are finding new ways of connecting through the technology of the internet. Our *Open Floor* dance teacher has organized a weekly class on zoom. Usually we meet in our village hall. Now dancers are joining from all over the world: eighty or ninety of us moving expressively to the music in our own home setting, appearing in a grid on the screen. Surprisingly it works and is enjoyable.

APRIL

I am settling down with no social contact except for zoom, facetime and the telephone. And speaking with my neighbour over the garden fence. These connections break the boundary of my absolute aloneness. I am isolated but not lonely.

The media is in an endless loop of comments and interviews about this deadly virus. SAGE stands for the Scientific Advisory Group for Emergencies: experts in fields as diverse as molecular biology, epidemiology, public health, behavioural psychology and statisticians from Institutions and Universities up and down the British Isles. These scientists are called upon by the government for their expertise, analysis and advice. There is a discrete separation of the different scientific disciplines themselves with varying edges to the expert knowledge. The boundaries blur through different interpretations of the data and daily statistics.

Not everyone is dying. But what we hear every day are the numbers: those infected with the virus, and those dying. Hundreds each day, amounting to thousands. The curves on the graphs are rising upwards. Pushing and crossing the lines representing the next zero mark, whether a hundred or a thousand deaths. The scientists and government are waiting for the graphs to *flatten out*. Tragic cases and heroic stories hit the headlines.

Coronavirus fills the airwaves. And the tone employs the language of war: fighting, conquering, defeating the killer virus. Here is a metaphor of battle endlessly extended and repeated. Illness and death are the enemies. Fear is their ally. The boundary of life into death with this language overwhelms the rarer voices which say *we have to learn how to live alongside this virus.* Language embraces separation rather than inclusion. This does not negate tragedy and anxiety but words to integrate our new reality might bring a more hopeful future. A different kind of truth which also embraces death as part of life.

There is also a war-time spirit of the population rallying to offer help. The supplies of Personal Protective Equipment for workers from doctors to porters in the NHS have been disastrously mismanaged. Staff on the *front-line* need to be properly protected with medical grade surgical masks and garments to provide a barrier around their own bodies, which will stop contamination from the Covid 19 patients they are treating.

Dressmakers up and down the country are making scrubs and masks. I receive a mask from a sister-in-law, made from a lovely green geometric patterned fabric, and now along with my blue rubber gloves, I secure the mask around my face for my few trips into the village.

Lockdown limits my personal freedoms, keeps me within the boundary of my house and garden, keeps me safe from virus, keeps me safe from inhaling tiny droplets of potential invasive pathogens. The boundary of my body is apparent but my invisible boundaries extend worldwide from the mind inside my head, from my heart inside my rib-cage, and from my invisible soul. This sense of myself connects me with all those I love, and the internet connects me with many of them as we zoom through the airwaves with online meetings. Many of us are on an upward learning curve of *zooming*: a new definition will surely enter the dictionary.

The wall of my skin remains untouched and I have not had a hug for weeks and I am fine. But I have taken on the fear when I am out of doors about not wanting to go near anyone. And not wanting any other person to come within the invisible two metre boundary. Never in my life have I gone out onto the street with my smile hidden behind a barrier.

MAY

During the midpoint of this month, there is a loosening of the restrictions around our personal boundaries. I visit my daughter and family for a short afternoon visit and receive the first hugs I have had for nine weeks. That touch with arms and hands around each other was so very familiar that the prohibitive boundary of *not touching* receded in a millisecond.

My three-year old grandson has understood the *lockdown* in his own way, suggesting *hoovering up the bugs*. He was canny enough to say, *You've done a sneaky visit, Grandma*. I wonder if he will lay down memories of this time when no visitors came to the house and crossed their threshold to come indoors.

How our society will emerge out of this global crisis is anyone's guess. Our future looks uncertain. As a species we are vulnerable to the challenge of climate change. We will have to encircle ourselves with living as well as we are able whilst acknowledging the interconnectedness of all our boundaries: looking after our bodies, living with each other respectfully, placing our feet on this earth with awareness. I only have questions with no answers.

Will I see my personal boundaries expand during my seventies? Will I want to travel on public transport? Maybe I will never return to Morocco and ride a camel again (see books 2 and 4). Maybe I will need to rein my boundaries tightly around myself.

Or maybe I will be prepared to take risks and have adventures for my remaining years.

Covid 19 has no respect for boundaries. Who could have known three months ago how our daily lives would shift beyond our imagination and keep us firmly within the boundaries of our home territory? Certainly in the short-term any meaning attached to boundaries has shifted for us all.

June 2020

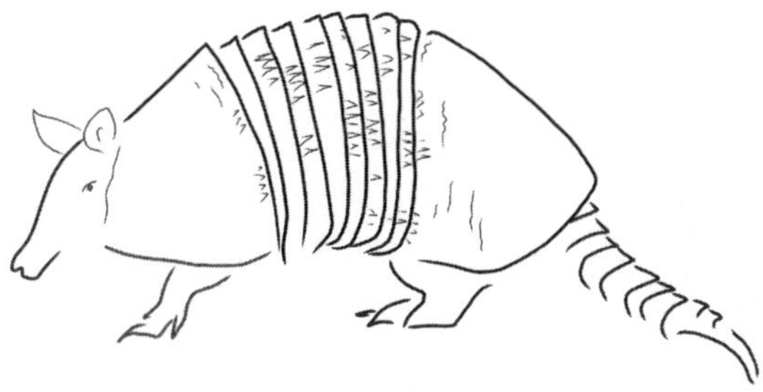

Appendix

NOTES

* marked by an asterisk in the text

CHAPTER 1– DREAM SNATCHER

Dream Writing: choose just one vivid image or scene from a dream (the dream snatch) and rewrite in the present tense. This will give you the feeling of bringing that scene to life, as if you are still in the dream. And then you can choose any number of creative therapeutic strategies for exploratory writing. See books 1 & 2 for the background to dream writing.

Lines in italics: *As for man, his days are as grass: as a flower of the field, so he flourisheth. For the wind passeth over it, and it is gone; and the place thereof shall know it no more.*

(Psalm 103 v. 15-6.)

Mental Illness: see *A Fox Crossed My Path: creative therapeutic writing on a depressive illness.* In this first book in the series, I show how writing about the mental illness episodes I suffered between the ages of 21 and 60 helped me integrate an Ill Self with my Well Self.

Spiralled Lives: When I wrote this poem I was totally unaware of the poem *Lament for Ignacio Sanchez Mejias* by Federico Garcia Lorca (1935) with the repeated lines of *at five in the afternoon*. It took someone else to point this out to me and then it felt uncanny. I knew I hadn't heard this poem about the death of a bull-fighter. And it then felt right to add the line about the time being *exactly five in the afternoon*. Because that was precisely the time my father died and I had the other lines about time all in place.

Separation from a parent: Attachment Theory, derived from the work of Dr John Bowlby (1907–1990), is an important part of the development of personality; his work focussed on babies and toddlers, drawing conclusions about the impact of early separation on adult lives.

Freewrite: a way of flowing with your writing; forgetting about grammar and any perceived right way of expressing language; allowing your pencil / pen to keep moving across the page, and saying what you really mean. Scribbling like this frees up your exploration, gives you a sense of adventure, and takes away any anxieties about writing. *Freewriting* is experiential and permissive, investing the writer with their own authority. A technique widely acknowledged in creative writing classes. It was made popular by Peter Elbow (b. 1935), Emeritus Professor of English, University of Massachusetts, USA (see: www.peterelbow.com) – author of *Writing Without Teachers* (1973), still in print. Accessing a stream of consciousness can be traced back to Freud's concept of free association. As a boy of fourteen, Freud, in turn, had been influenced by the books of Ludwig Börne (1786–1837) which made a lasting impression on him right into adulthood. Ernest Jones in his biography of Freud, points out that Börne wrote an essay, *The Art of Becoming an Original Writer in Three Days* (1823), advocating writing everything down and this 'startling proposal had sunk into Freud's mind' . . . 'stimulating him to give his patients' thoughts free play' (Jones 1967, p.219).

Fritz Perls (1893–1970): one of the innovators of the *Human Potential Movement* which made psychotherapy far more accessible. He was the father of what has evolved into Gestalt Therapy as we know it today and used the word *gestalt* meaning 'whole' in his native German.

Ann Faraday: is the author of two influential books, *Dream Power: the use of dreams in everyday life* (1972) and later *The Dream Game* (1975). British born, she took her PhD in dream research at University College, London and later settled in Australia. Her books are still in print. This quote comes from an undated online post, 'Through psychotherapy and dream-work ... [I was led] on to even deeper archetypal encounters which expanded *the boundaries of self* into the greater collective psyche of humankind.' (italics mine). *An Account of the "Realization of Emptiness"* by Dr. Ann Faraday www.sped2work.tripod.com (accessed 23 March 2020).

CHAPTER 2 – SHIFTING BOUNDARIES

Dylan Thomas (1914–1953): came from a very large Welsh family, lived in Wales and London. A prolific writer, part of the London literary circle, always considered to be original. *Under Milk Wood* (a play for voices) is one of his most famous works. The villanelle *Do not go gentle into that good night* was written in 1951 for his dying father. Dylan, not yet forty, died the following year during a lecture tour of America. His death may have been due to less than good medical care, his own self-neglect and a history of respiratory disease, although the stories persisted about his excessive drinking.

King Solomon: son of King David, lived in the tenth century BC. The judgement of Solomon can be found in the Old Testament (1 Kings 3: 16-28). Two women came to the King saying they each had given birth to a son but one had died. Both claimed the living baby. Solomon called for his sword, *Divide the child in half and give each mother one half,* he said. One mother agreed to this solution, the other said, *Give her the child,* begging him not to slay the living baby. Solomon judged she was the real mother and gave her the boy.

Virginia Woolf: coined the phrase 'undiscovered countries' in her essay *On Being Ill* (1926).

Jewish Religion: as much as anything else Judaism is about cultural identity, as well as an affiliation to a religion going back three thousand years to Moses and the Ten Commandments. There are a range of belief systems within Judaism ranging from the orthodox (ultra conservative) through reform to the liberal with an anglicised liturgy. The transition from Judaism to Christianity took place in the first few centuries after Christ was crucified. With the symbolic eating of the bread and wine during the Passover / the Last Supper evolving into the Eucharist.

Clock: my etymological dictionary (nineteenth century) draws a distinctive link to Celtic languages, Anglo-Saxon and Latinate words. *Clag, clog, cluega* all point to the sounding of a bell, originally used to mark time. Time has been measured since the ancient Egyptians devised the sun dial for day-light hours and water clocks for night: vessels lined with markings as water trickled out of a small hole. Hours may have been approximate for centuries. And inventions ever driven to greater accuracy until our present day when we have precision devices to measure time to the fraction of a second.

Stephen Hawking: (1942–2018) Professor of Mathematics and Theoretical Physics (Cambridge University). His aim was to understand the Universe; to uncover a unifying theory of everything. In *A Brief History of Time* (1988), he outlines the complexity of physics, mathematics and theories of relativity and time. But he starts by asking the questions any of us might ask about the universe. Read an article by Peter Guzzardi, his editor, describing their first meeting and his experience publishing the book, which has sold millions of copies worldwide for readers without a scientific background. See: www.theguardian.com 14 March 2018 (accessed: 2 January 2020).

Big Bang Theory: the accepted (but sometimes disputed scientific model) of how the universe may have started from what is called a 'singularity' of hot, small matter which exploded and expanded and continues to expand. Time itself is probably reckoned to have started, Hawking indicated, with the Big Bang ten thousand million years ago.

Black Hole: a phenomenon in space time when the light rays of a dying star are tipping inwards from the surface with more and more gravitational pull, so strong that no matter or electromagnetic radiation like light can escape.

Northern Lights: the sun provides the light show with its positive and negative particles shooting out from its magnetic field; these are carried on solar winds to come up against, whirl around and interact with the earth's own magnetic field and oxygen in complex spirals, releasing energy to form the colours of the aurora.

Mind Maps: sometimes called spider patterns, cluster maps. A very useful way of thinking diagrammatically and flexibly in the round, using only key words. I came across Tony Buzan's book *Use Your Head* (to accompany a BBC television series in 1974) in my twenties and have been using mind maps ever since for anything and everything which needs planning.

CHAPTER 3 – WALL FICTIONS

Martin Buber (1878–1965): Jewish philosopher, political activist and educator. In *I and Thou* (1923), he defines the human individual in terms of relationship: both distancing and relating to 'it' and an 'other'. Born in Vienna and dying in Jerusalem, he was an architect of Zionism: advocating a bi-national Israeli-Palestinian unified state, which in no way should violate 'the fundamental rights of the Arab people' (in the foreword to *On Zion: The History of an Idea*).

Naïve Voice: phrase for my inner child's simple style of language. I choose to use the word *naïve* because I still maintain my adult self whilst I write simply. I use minimal punctuation and often only lower case letters.

Henri Rousseau (1844–1910): self-taught and initially ridiculed by critics. Nevertheless he had a following amongst the avant-garde French painters who saw genius in his style: colourful, vibrant, complex yet naïve. Although he never left France, he is best known for his jungle scenes.

Extended Metaphor: a metaphor is a literary device which compares one thing with another. Often an abstract concept expressed through a concrete image. An extended metaphor will achieve this more fully through several sentences or a sequence of paragraphs.

Wall Writing: a version of this piece originally appeared in *Writing Routes* in the chapter *Relationships,* published by Jessica Kingsley Publications, edited by Gillie Bolton.

Berlin Wall (also known as the Iron Curtain) 1961–1990: built after the war to separate the Eastern bloc population from a still feared post-fascist Germany. In 1989, as communism was losing its hold, separation between East and West Germany was eased. People crossed and smashed the wall; a year later it came down, paving the way for reunification.

Great Wall of China: built over two thousand years ago by a Chinese Emperor to mark the northern boundary of his lands to protect the territory from enemy attacks.

Hadrian's Wall: built by the Emperor Hadrian in Britain to mark the North-West extreme of the Roman Empire in the second century. The Roman soldiers regulated the passage of Scottish peasants from the unconquered lands to the north.

The Western (or Wailing) Wall: still standing from the holy site of the original temple built by King Solomon during his reign of Israel in the tenth century BC. Access to the wall has been denied, granted and caused friction and hostility over the last two millennia to the Jewish peoples. I stood before it when I was 19, after the Six Day War in 1967 reclaimed access to Old Jerusalem. My memory is of dovenning (praying and swaying) men, with shawls wrapped around their shoulders. Images we see on our television screens.

West Bank Barrier: the controversial and hideous concrete and barbed wire construction runs for hundreds of miles, disrupting Palestinian agricultural land and villages whilst stating its purpose is to prevent Palestinian attacks on Israel. Started in 2002, and built to provide a no-man buffer zone between the citizens of Israel and the Palestinians. Some of those who have built the barrier and idealised Zionism are the descendants of Jews who had fled Nazi Germany before or during World War Two.

CHAPTER 4 – TABLECLOTH TALK

Literary Fiction: deals with themes worthy of publication. The author has a bigger picture in mind when tackling the writing which would finally be considered of merit.

Author's Voice: the job of the writer is to allow the story to be told and keep themselves off the page. That means personal opinions that do not belong to the characters or the narrator. Nevertheless the author's style may well show a distinct style of authority. The roots of the words: *author, authority, authentic* all go back to the Greek meaning of *genuine*, the power to influence, an originator.

Narrator's Voice: every story has a narrator and the writer has to find out who that narrator is when they are telling the story. It is a question of perspective and remaining consistent to that voice. It might be a character in the first person, giving only that viewpoint. Or maybe the narrator moves around varying viewpoints with the voices of different characters. Or there may be an all-knowing, omniscient narrator who has an overview of the fiction and knows everything there is to know about characters and events. And takes the reader into their confidence. Unless s/he is an unreliable narrator and the reader sees more clearly than the narrator what is happening.

Also see: *Top 10 unreliable narrators* by Sarah Pinborough.
The Guardian 4 January 2017 (accessed: 11 March 2020)

Quote: Quite by chance, I discovered that a short audio play, *This Gun That I Have in My Right Hand Is Loaded,* was written by the actor Timothy West (born: 1934) in 1959. A satire of bad radio drama with over-explanatory dialogue and typical mistakes was written as a guide of how not to write. www.englishwordplay.com (accessed: 29 June 2019).

Max Planck Institute for Psycholinguistics: lecture (2015) by Simeon Floyd in Antwerp on expressions of gratitude in eight cultures around the world. See: *Terribly sorry – but Britain's famed politeness may be a myth* by Lynne Murphy.

The Guardian 26 May 2018 (accessed: 7 April 2019)

References

Austen, J. [1816] (1953). *Emma*. London: Collins.

Bolton, G. (ed.) (2008). *Dying, Bereavement and the Healing Arts*. London: Jessica Kingsley Publishers.

Bolton, G., Field V., Thompson, K. (2011). *Writing Routes: A Resource Handbook of Therapeutic Writing*. London: Jessica Kingsley Publishers.

Buber, M. [1952] (1985). *On Zion: The History of an Idea*. Edinburgh: T & T Clark.

Buzan, T. (1974). *Use Your Head*. London: British Broadcasting Corporation.

Elbow, P. [1973] (1998). *Writing Without Teachers*. New York: Oxford University Press.

Faraday, A. (1972). *Dream Power: The use of dreams in everyday life*. London: Hodder and Stoughton.

Gilbert, E. (2015). *Big Magic: Creative Living Beyond Fear*. London: Bloomsbury.

Hawking, S. (1988). *A Brief History of Time*. London: Bantam Press.

Jones, E. [1953] (1967). *The Life and Work of Sigmund Freud*. London: Pelican Books.

Keats, J. (1819). *Ode On A Grecian Urn*. In *Library of World Poetry*. New York: Avenil Books.

Mauss, M. [1950] (2002). *The Gift: The form and reason for exchange in archaic societies*. London and New York: Routledge Classics.

Ravenscroft, S. (2017). *A Macat Analysis: Martin Buber's I & Thou*. London: Routledge.

Skeat W. (1893). *An Etymological Dictionary of the English Language*. Oxford: The Clarendon Press.

Suswin, M. (2017). *A Fox Crossed My Path: creative therapeutic writing on a depressive illness*. Sussex: Cabin Press.

Suswin, M. (2018). *Love & Loss: creative therapeutic writing on relationships*. Sussex: Cabin Press.

Suswin, M. (2019). *Rope Mates: creative therapeutic writing on companionship for writers*. Sussex: Cabin Press.

Thomas, A. (2008). *Thinking About Memoir*. New York: Sterling Publishing.

Woolf, V. [1931] (1966). *The Waves*. Middlesex, England: Penguin Modern Classics.

Woolf, V. [1930] (1981). *On Being Ill* in *The Moment and Other Essays*. London: Hogarth Press.

Index

Boxes for Exercises or Information are in bold

for your own mind maps,
notes and scribbles

for your own mind maps,
notes and scribbles

Praise for the Series

A Fox Crossed My Path: creative therapeutic writing on a depressive illnesses

Monca Suswin shows how she has wrestled with mental illness (the scavenger fox of the title), and how she has searched for the reasons it visited her. ... [This] is an exploration of how different forms of writing can become containers for traumatic experiences, and in so doing lay them to rest. ... The honesty and integrity of the book is what makes it compelling – depressive illness is in no way romanticised, but is described unflinchingly, and as far as is possible, with acceptance.

Rachel Cole, Frogmore Press

Love & Loss: creative therapeutic writing on relationships

What is immediately apparent in reading this work is the accessible and honest telling, from an experiential base. And the invitation for the reader is to write and in this way cultivate personal wisdom. The exercises are fun, clever, and entertaining. This book, if used to reflect and do one's own writing, will certainly bring personal insight and support the cultivation of self-trust – which is exactly what is needed to trust love.

Dr Reinekke Lengelle, author of *Writing the Self in Bereavement: A Story of Love, Spousal Loss and Resilience* (Routledge 2021)

Rope Mates: creative therapeutic writing on companionship for writers

This compassionate and permissive guide to therapeutic writing, is a personal, but professionally grounded celebration of the invaluable support writers can receive from significant companions on their creative journey. *Rope Mates* encompasses the spiritual, psychological, intellectual and lyrical dimensions of creative writing, and in so doing eloquently distils the work of a lifetime.

Naomi Foyle, author of *Adamantine* and *The Gaia Chronicles*